7-9-75

The Revolutionary Potential of the Working Class

Ernest Mandel and George Novack

PATHFINDER PRESS
NEW YORK

"The Unfolding of the New Radicalization in the United States"
appeared in the February 1974 *International Socialist Review* under the title "The Reradicalization of American Politics."
"Revolutionary Strategy in the Imperialist Countries" originally appeared in 1970 as a Merit pamphlet (published by Pathfinder Press).
"Workers Under Neo-Capitalism" and "Can American Workers Make a Socialist Revolution?" originally appeared in *International Socialist Review*, November-December 1968 and January-February 1969, and were reprinted as a Merit pamphlet in 1969.

Library of Congress Catalog Card No. 74-75357
Manufactured in the United States of America

Pathfinder Press, Inc.
410 West Street
New York, N.Y. 10014

CONTENTS

Introduction   5

Ernest Mandel:

WORKERS UNDER NEO-CAPITALISM   13

REVOLUTIONARY STRATEGY IN THE
IMPERIALIST COUNTRIES   29

George Novack:

CAN AMERICAN WORKERS MAKE A
SOCIALIST REVOLUTION?   40

THE UNFOLDING OF THE NEW
RADICALIZATION IN THE
UNITED STATES   65

PARIS, MAY 1968

Sign on plant gate: "Factory occupied." Chalked slogans at left demand: "Schools to the students. Factories to the workers."

INTRODUCTION

Long before Marx, the injustices of class-divided society provoked some thinkers to develop socialist or quasi-socialist ideas. Why should there be a few rich and many poor? Why should there be wars of plunder against colonial peoples and among the rulers of competing empires? Why should ruthless exploiters be allowed to keep their stolen wealth? Why shouldn't everyone join in a cooperative effort and share equally in what they produce?

But these ideas were mostly confined to a handful of radical philosophers and impractical dreamers. Some philanthropists actually experimented with utopian colonies, hoping that enlightened rulers would follow their example — but the rulers preferred to keep their privileges and power.

In the early nineteenth century, the factory system began to revolutionize industry. A new class began to take shape on a large scale — the proletariat, made up of people whose living comes from wages — and a new, practical kind of socialist thinking arose with it.

In 1848 Marx and Engels published their famous pamphlet, *The Communist Manifesto,* and put the goal of a socialist future on a scientific and political basis, not just a moral one. *The Manifesto* traced the evolution of economic forces that had produced capitalism and concluded that socialism was on the agenda as the next stage in social development. Capitalism itself was laying the foundation for the kind of productive system that could meet all human needs efficiently. However, the dynamics of a system dominated by profiteers made it irrational and subject to crises. Periodically it was hardly able to function at all, let alone for the public good. But at the same time, capitalism was creating the force that would reorganize production on a collective basis — the workers.

This growing class of producers, Marx and Engels explained, had both the incentive and the power to take control of industry and transform it. The working class had no vested interest in capitalist society. It had no special privileges or property to defend. On the contrary, its only hope lay in ending exploitation and running society for the benefit of the majority. For the working class socialism was not an idle dream but a vital historical necessity.

Furthermore, the workers were in a strategic position. They were concentrated in the very heart of the system, the cities and the factories. Capitalism itself was organizing them into an industrial army, a giant mass that had to cooperate to carry out its daily work. This gave the workers a glimpse of their own social power, their ability to act together to produce — or to stop production. Marx and Engels pointed out in the *Manifesto* that strikes and efforts to form unions were spreading almost as fast as industry itself.

The movement of Marxist socialism, based on the historic interests and social power of the working class, soon became a force in its own right as more and more of the workers themselves adopted its ideas. By the end of the nineteenth century the Second International, founded by Engels, had organized millions of workers into socialist parties. Marxism became the dominant ideology of the labor movement in Western Europe and began to spread even to the politically backward United States.

In 1871 the workers of Paris actually seized power, organized a government of their own, and started to administer production and distribution. Although the Paris Commune was soon crushed by outside military force, its example helped inspire the revolutionary Marxists of Russia in 1917 — the Bolsheviks led by Lenin and Trotsky. Their establishment of a lasting workers' state won new millions to Marxism around the world. The Bolsheviks proved that socialist revolution was a realistic project, that the working class and its allies could take power from the profiteers and warmakers and start to build a cooperative society.

But despite the crises and revolutionary upsurges that shook the world in the aftermath of World War I, in the nineteen-thirties, and again after World War II, capitalism was able to survive in all the major industrial countries — the decisive arena of the international class struggle. Its ideological defenders were thus given a new lease on life. Marxism's ability to analyze, anticipate, and guide the process of social change was put in question. The possibility — and desirability — of the workers' taking power was denied by one leading thinker after another.

In the United States especially, the long prosperity that followed World War II seemed to have absorbed the workers totally into the system. When a new generation of radicals, composed mainly of students, began to challenge racism and imperialist wars in the early nineteen-sixties, they looked on the working class as anything but an ally.

While rejecting much of capitalist ideology, these radicals tended to accept the myth that America's workers were so prosperous and contented that they had become simply a blue-collar branch

6

of the middle class. No longer really proletarians, the workers were pictured as partners in capitalism who saw its interests as their own.

These ideas were further developed and popularized by the sociologist C. Wright Mills and the philosopher Herbert Marcuse. They and their disciples in the leadership of the Students for a Democratic Society (SDS) were the most prominent figures in what became known as the New Left.

Most of these radicals considered themselves socialists, at least in some vague way. But they rejected the Marxism of the traditional left (as they understood it) and denied that there was a revolutionary potential in the working class. This led them to a search for all sorts of substitute forces and shortcut tactics, which finally wound up in a political dead end.

As the New Left fell apart, the most serious young revolutionaries began to take another, closer look at Marxist ideas. But they demanded to know: Is there a variety of Marxism that can combine the revolutionary traditions of the Bolsheviks with today's special circumstances? How do Marxists explain the apparent retreat of the working class — and can they offer any cogent reasons for believing that the workers will again move to the front lines of revolutionary struggle? And even if the workers can become radicalized, do they retain the kind of potential power needed to unseat the owners of the arsenal of capitalism, the United States?

These are the questions discussed by the authors of this book. They reject the anti-Marxist and anti-working class theories of the New Left and take a fresh look at the relevance of Marxist concepts in the modern world.

The authors, among the leading contemporary Marxist teachers, are exponents of the ideas and methods of Leon Trotsky, who defended Bolshevik principles against their perversion by Stalin. They can offer this generation an unfalsified and revolutionary Marxism, free of the undemocratic and reformist corruption that repels so many young rebels from the traditional "Communist" and "Socialist" parties.

Ernest Mandel of Belgium is one of the world's outstanding Marxist economists, best known for his two-volume *Marxist Economic Theory*, which included a pioneering analysis of capitalism's evolution after the depression of the thirties. Mandel's works have been published in at least a dozen languages from French to Japanese.

George Novack's writings on history and philosophy have both explained and enriched the Marxist heritage. His books include *An Introduction to the Logic of Marxism* and *Humanism and Socialism*. He has also played a prominent role in the defense of civil liberties, starting in the thirties with the Scottsboro case and the exposure of the Moscow trials.

Mandel's two contributions make up the first part of this book. They examine the underlying trends in Western society today and reveal that modern capitalism — far from escaping the tendencies noted in the nineteenth century by Marx — is in fact providing new confirmation of them. Mandel pins down just what the working class is, how it has changed — and how the behavior of both the "new" and "old" components of the working class points in a revolutionary direction.

Mandel and Novack draw important conclusions from the revolutionary crisis in France in May and June of 1968. Here was a demonstration of the role the student movement could play as a catalyst, as well as the limits of its power in a showdown with the capitalist state. At the same time, the May-June events gave a graphic example of the workers' ability to stand up, begin to shake off their reformist leaders, and go into action in an advanced industrial country.

In the end, the French general strike, the greatest in labor's history, failed. There was no revolutionary organization of sufficient size and influence to lead it to victory. The main working-class party, the Communist Party, reached an agreement with de Gaulle and settled for a few token reforms. But in its wake the French uprising left a whole generation of radical youth — workers and students both — with the experience of a revolutionary workers' mobilization in their lifetimes. Its impact was immediate and international.

The New Left theorists lost most of their credibility and their followers after the 1968 worker-student uprising in France. But not all the young radicals were convinced, especially in the United States. They have seen workers acting as a powerful radical force in France, Italy, Britain, Chile, Argentina, Mexico — but the United States remains the great exception. Even revolutionaries in other countries who accept the ideas of Marxism have wondered whether the American workers shouldn't be written off as hopeless — at least the majority, the white workers.

George Novack's first essay tackles this question. It explains the underlying causes of the conservatism of American labor, and also brings to the surface the strategic factors that give the American workers a greater potential power today than ever before.

Ironically, many of the New Leftists in the United States reacted with just as much shortsightedness and superficiality to the French general strike as they had to the preceding temporary lull in proletarian radicalism. They performed a sudden ideological somersault, declared the working class to be the only layer of society that mattered in developing a revolutionary movement, and tossed the independent struggles of students, blacks, and women into the closet like a discarded toy.

This school of thought, now common among young revolutionaries, is what Marxists have labeled "workerism." In its own way it downgrades the real potential of the working class for developing political consciousness, and it fails to understand the diverse components and stages of the real revolutionary process.

While recognizing the working class as the central force opposing capitalism, the workerists ignore or downgrade the role of all other forces — including the workers' potential allies. Seeing the decisive role the proletariat will play in the long run and in the showdown, they close their eyes to the reality of the present situation in the United States.

Yet in America today many of the opportunities to spread anticapitalist consciousness and struggle are found among the rebellious masses in the colleges and high schools, the oppressed nationalities, and the women's movement. Even more important, it is among such groups that new individuals can be won in significant numbers to the revolutionary movement, educated, organized, and tested in the heat of political activity — to be ready to participate in and help lead the coming struggles of the radicalized workers.

Far from being irrelevant to the working class, as the workerists claim, the demands and actions of these groups will provide both an impetus and an auxiliary force to the rebellion of the workers. The radicalization of the working class includes the radicalization of working-class housewives and high-school students, of working women, of Afro-American, Puerto Rican, and Chicano workers, of GIs and unemployed youth. It is not just job-related economic issues that can provoke the working class — the big majority of the American people — to act against the system.

The workers of the United States are about 40 percent women and at least 10 percent black. Millions more are Chicanos, Puerto Ricans, and members of other oppressed minorities. More than a fifth of the labor force are under 25, and a very large percentage of this age group are former college students who have been exposed to the political ferment on the campuses. As this ferment extends more and more into the high schools, it can affect almost the entire future working class.

Not only will their example help pave the way for political struggle by the workers; the preliminary radicalization of blacks, Latinos, women, and young people will actually intensify the revolutionary potential of the working class as a whole. The most oppressed are often the most advanced elements among the workers and their allies. When they raise their special demands in the context of a spreading working-class rebellion, the combination will strike deeper at capitalism than economic demands alone. Special forms of oppression such as racism and the subordination of women are basic to the capitalist system's survival.

That is why anyone who hopes to understand or participate in coming revolutionary struggles must carefully study the dynamics of the movements that have unfolded so far. In the second of two articles on the American situation that make up half of this book, George Novack traces the roots and evolution of the radicalization of the sixties and seventies. This varied and unique radicalization is not just a temporary diversion while we wait for economic crises to reawaken the workers; as this article shows, it is helping to set the stage for this awakening.

Mandel and Novack largely base their case for optimism about the workers' potential on theoretical grounds, on the experiences of the workers' movement from the eighteen-forties to the present, and on the deep processes at work in the advanced capitalist countries. They apply Marxist theory about the proletariat to today's conditions, demonstrating its continued relevance and the revolutionary perspective that flows from it.

But in the long run, theory must be verified in practice. This is itself one of the keystones of Marxist thought. In that sense the answer is still incomplete; only a successful socialist revolution led by the working class in one of the advanced capitalist countries — above all in the United States — can once and for all refute the skeptics who deny the combative and creative power of the workers.

Recent events provide some important factual evidence that can be added to arguments based on analysis and past experience. There are growing signs of a questioning of authority and an openness to militant action in the ranks of labor — even among some of the white workers who enjoy union protection and a relatively high standard of living.

As George Novack points out, and as polls confirmed, resentment against the government caused by the Vietnam war, and later by the revelations of corruption and foul play connected with Watergate, became general throughout the U. S. population — including the majority of workers — in the late sixties and early seventies. At the same time the growing difficulties of the economy, and the government's obvious collusion with the corporations in rigging price increases and artificial shortages, began to spark protests among working people.

Outstanding examples included the massive meat boycott and anti-inflation demonstrations in the spring of 1973 and the strike and highway blockades by independent truck owner-drivers in the

10

winter of 1973-74. These were largely spontaneous and sporadic. The conservative bureaucrats who dominate the labor movement kept them from achieving more massive striking power and support. But these actions gave a hint of the bottled-up potential for rebellion in the American working class.

They also gave a clue to the trailblazing role played by the radicalization of other social layers. When striking truckers were interviewed by the press, some of them pointed to the student protests against the Vietnam war as the example they had followed.

The late sixties and early seventies also saw one example after another of the direct impact the radicalization was having on people who belonged to both the working class and one of the groups that had begun to struggle. The black caucuses in the auto union, the Chicano nationalist aspect of the United Farm Workers organizing drive, the rebellion of young workers in the Lordstown General Motors plant, and the sudden rise of a movement of trade union women fighting for their rights both as workers and as women — all these underscore the simmering discontent among the workers and, at the same time, the importance of the radicalization of women, Afro-Americans, Chicanos, and students.

These early stirrings of protest among working people have shared an important feature. They have tended to focus their demands and complaints directly on the government that represents corporate power as a whole. This speaks well for the broader and deeper anticapitalist consciousness that will emerge among the masses as the radicalization unfolds.

One of the articles in this book has a rather dramatic history which in its own way confirms the relevance of revolutionary Marxism and its challenge to present social conditions.

Ernest Mandel had been invited to give the keynote address at a gathering sponsored by the Bertrand Russell Peace Foundation and the Socialist Scholars Conference in New York on November 29, 1969. That talk — "Revolutionary Strategy in the Imperialist Countries" — had to be heard via tape recording because the Nixon administration barred Mandel from entering the United States.

Under the McCarran-Walter Act of 1952 the Justice Department has the power to issue such bans on an arbitrary basis. Anyone on its secret list cannot enter the United States without permission of the attorney general. This permission had been granted to Mandel in 1962 and 1968.

The hard line of the Nixon administration on excluding Mandel in 1969 caused a storm of protest in the press and academic community which led to a public split in Nixon's own cabinet. Secretary of State William Rogers realized that the ban on Mandel could not be sold to the public with McCarthy-era rhetoric, and he

11

recommended reversing it. Attorney General John Mitchell, Nixon's closest associate at the time, refused to bend. Although Mitchell has since been discredited and incriminated, Mandel still cannot visit the U. S. — and has also been barred from Switzerland, France, Australia, New Zealand, and West Germany.

What these reactionary rulers fear is precisely what they cannot stop — the spread of Marxist ideas and their fusion with a resurgent working-class movement. Such ideas are gaining ground because they are proving once again their superiority in analyzing social forces — and their ability to show a new generation of revolutionaries what to expect and what to do.

March 1974   JESSE SMITH

Ernest Mandel

WORKERS UNDER NEO-CAPITALISM

This paper was delivered at the 1968 Socialist Scholars Conference, held on September 7 at Rutgers University.

In the history of class society, the situation of each social class is a unique combination of stability and change. The structure remains the same; conjunctural features are often profoundly modified.

There is a tremendous difference both in standard of living and in social environment between the slave on the patriarchal Greek farms of the sixth century B. C., the slave on Sicilian plantations in the first century B. C., and a clerical or handicraft slave in Rome or the south of France in the fourth century A. D. Nonetheless all three of these were slaves, and the identity of their social status is undeniable. A nobleman living at the court of Louis XV did not have very much in common with a lord of the manor in Normandy or Burgundy seven centuries earlier — except that both lived on surplus labor extracted from the peasantry through feudal or semi-feudal institutions.

When we look at the history of the modern proletariat, whose direct ancestors were the unattached and uprooted wage earners in the medieval towns and the vagabonds of the 16th century — so strikingly described by that great novel from my country *Till Eulenspiegel* — we notice the same combination of structural stability and conjunctural change. The proletarian condition is, in a nutshell, the lack of access to means of production or means of subsistence which, in a society of generalized commodity production, forces the proletarian to sell his labor-power. In exchange for this labor-power he receives a wage which then enables him to acquire the means of consumption necessary for satisfying his own needs and those of his family.

This is the structural definition of the wage earner, the proletarian. From it necessarily flows a certain relationship to his work, to the products of his work, and to his overall situation in society, which can be summarized by the catchword "alienation." But there does not follow from this structural definition any necessary conclusions as to the level

13

of his consumption, the price he receives for his labor-power, the extent of his needs or the degree to which he can satisfy them. The only basic interrelationship between structural stability of status and conjunctural fluctuations of income and consumption is a very simple one: Does the wage, whether high or low, whether in miserable Calcutta slums or in the much publicized comfortable suburbs of the American megalopolis, enable the proletarian to free himself from the social and economic obligation to sell his labor-power? Does it enable him to go into business on his own account?

Occupational statistics testify that this is no more open to him today than a hundred years ago. Nay, they confirm that the part of the active population in today's United States which is forced to sell its labor-power is much higher than it was in Britain when Karl Marx wrote *Das Kapital*, not to speak of the United States on the eve of the American Civil War.

Nobody will deny that the picture of the working class under neo-capitalism would be highly oversimplified if it were limited to featuring only this basic structural stability of the proletarian condition. In general, though, Marxists who continue to stress the basic revolutionary role of today's proletariat in Western imperialist society avoid that pitfall. It is rather their critics who are in error, who commit the opposite error in fact of concentrating exclusively on conjunctural changes in the situation of the working class, thereby forgetting those fundamental structural elements which have not changed.

I do not care very much for the term "neo-capitalism" which is ambiguous, to say the least. When one speaks about the "neo-reformism" of the Communist parties in the West, one means, of course, that they are basically reformist; but when the term "neo-socialists" was used in the thirties and early forties to define such dubious figures as Marcel Deat or Henri de Man, one meant rather that they had stopped being socialists. Some European politicians and sociologists speak about "neo-capitalism" in the sense that society has shed some of the basic characteristics of capitalism. I deny this most categorically, and therefore attach to the term "neo-capitalism" the opposite connotation: a society which has all the basic elements of classical capitalism.

Nevertheless I am quite convinced that starting either with the great depression of 1929-32 or with the second world war, capitalism entered into a third stage in its development, which is as different from monopoly capitalism or imperialism described by Lenin, Hilferding and others as monopoly capitalism was different from classical 19th century laissez-faire capitalism. We have to give this child a name; all other names proposed seem even less acceptable than "neo-capitalism." "State monopoly capitalism," the term used in the Soviet Union and the "official" Communist parties, is very misleading because it implies a degree of independence of the state which, to my mind, does

14

not at all correspond to present-day reality. On the contrary, I would say that today the state is a much more direct instrument for guaranteeing monopoly surplus profits to the strongest private monopolies than it ever was in the past. The German term *Spaetkapitalismus* seems interesting, but simply indicates a time sequence and is difficult to translate into several languages. So until somebody comes up with a better name—and this is a challenge to you, friends!—we will stick for the time being to "neo-capitalism."

We shall define neo-capitalism as this latest stage in the development of monopoly capitalism in which a combination of factors—accelerated technological innovation, permanent war economy, expanding colonial revolution—have transferred the main source of monopoly surplus profits from the colonial countries to the imperialist countries themselves and made the giant corporations both more independent and more vulnerable.

More independent, because the enormous accumulation of monopoly surplus profits enables these corporations, through the mechanisms of price investment and self-financing, and with the help of a constant buildup of sales costs, distribution costs and research and development expenses, to free themselves from that strict control by banks and finance capital which characterized the trusts and monopolies of Hilferding's and Lenin's epoch. More vulnerable, because of shortening of the life cycle of fixed capital, the growing phenomenon of surplus capacity, the relative decline of customers in non-capitalist milieus and, last but not least, the growing challenge of the non-capitalist forces in the world (the so-called socialist countries, the colonial revolution and, potentially at least, the working class in the metropolis) has implanted even in minor fluctuations and crises the seeds of dangerous explosions and total collapse.

For these reasons, neo-capitalism is compelled to embark upon all those well-known techniques of economic programming, of deficit financing and pump-priming, of incomes policies and wage freezing, of state subsidizing of big business and state guaranteeing of monopoly surplus profit, which have become permanent features of most Western economies over the last 20 years. What has emerged is a society which appears both as more prosperous and more explosive than the situation of imperialist countries 30 years ago.

It is a society in which the basic contradictions of capitalism have not been overcome, in which some of them reach unheard-of dimensions, in which powerful long-term forces are at work to blow up the system. I will mention here in passing only some of these forces: The growing crisis of the international monetary system; the trend towards a generalized economic recession in the whole capitalist world; the trend to restrict or suppress the basic democratic freedoms of the working class, in the first place, free play of wage bargaining; the trend toward deep and growing dissatisfaction of producers and consumers with a system which forces them to lose more and more time producing and consuming more and more commodities which give less and less satisfaction and stifle more and more basic human needs, emotions and aspirations; the contradictions between the accumulation of wasteful "wealth" in the West and the hunger and misery of the colonial peoples; the contradictions between the immense creative and productive potentialities of science and automation and the destructive horror of nuclear war in the shadow of which we are forced to live permanently — these epitomize the basic contradictions of today's capitalism.

The question has been posed: Hasn't the role of the working class been fundamentally changed in this changed environment? Hasn't the long-term high level of employment and the rising real wage undercut any revolutionary potential of the working class? Isn't it changing in composition, and more and more divorced from the productive process, as a result of growing automation? Don't its relations with other social layers, such as white-collar workers, technicians, intellectuals, students, undergo basic modifications?

Affirmative answers to these questions lead to political conclusions of far-reaching consequence. For some, the stability of the capitalist system in the West cannot be shaken any more, a theory which is nicely fitted to nourish a more material interest and psychological urge of adaptation to that system. For others, that stability could be shaken only from outside: first of all, from the non-industrialized regions of the world — the so-called villages, to repeat Lin Piao's formula — which will have to be revolutionized before revolts could again be envisaged in the imperialist countries themselves (Lin Piao's cities). Others, while not questioning the basic instability of neo-capitalism, see no positive outcome at all because they believe that the system is able to drug and paralyze its victims. Finally, there are those who believe that neo-capitalism raises its gravediggers from within its bosom but see these gravediggers coming from the groups of outcasts: national and racial minorities, superexploited sections of the population, revolutionary students, the new youth vanguard. All these conclusions share in common the elimination of the proletariat of metropolitan countries from the central role in the worldwide struggle against imperialism and capitalism.

It would be easy to limit oneself to stating an obvious fact: All these theories spring from a premature rationalization of a given situation, the fact that the Western proletariat has receded into the background of the world revolutionary struggle for the past 20 years, between 1948 and 1968. Now that the French May 1968 revolution has shown this phenomenon and period to be a temporary one, we should rather put at the top of the agenda a discussion of revolutionary perspectives in the West from now on.

Such an answer, valid though it may be, would remain insufficient and incomplete. For some of the theories we have just mentioned, while being obvious rationalizations of the *fait accompli*, have enough sophistication and candor not to limit themselves to description pure and simple. They try to draw conclusions about the declining revolutionary role of the proletariat in the West from changes introduced into the very fabric of neo-capitalist society by technological, economic, social and cultural transformations of historic proportions and importance. So we have to meet these arguments on their own ground, and critically reexamine the dynamics of working class struggles, consciousness and revolutionary potential against the background of the changes which neo-capitalism has effected in the classical *modus operandi* of the capitalist system.

Our starting point must be the same as that adopted not only by Karl Marx but also by the classical school of political economy: the study of the place human labor occupies in the economic life of contemporary monopoly capitalism. Three basic facts immediately demand our attention in that respect.

First, contemporary production and distribution of material wealth is more than ever based upon modern industry and the factory. Indeed, one could say that the third industrial revolution at one and the same time both reduces industrial labor in the factory as a result of growing automation and increases industrial labor on a vast scale in agriculture, distribution, the service industries and administration. For the automation revolution must be seen as a vast movement of *industrialization* of these different sectors of economic activity, both economically and socially. We shall have to draw important conclusions from this trend. But what stands out is the fact that industrial labor in the broadest sense of the word — men forced to sell their labor-power to the manufacturing, cotton-growing, data-processing or dream-producing factory! — more than ever occupies the central place in the economy's structure.

Second, whatever the increase in consumption of the working class may have been, neo-capitalism hasn't modified in any sense whatsoever the basic nature of work in a capitalist society as alienated labor. One could even say that in the same way as automation extends the industrialization process into every single corner of economic life, it likewise universalizes alienation to an extent Marx and Engels could only have dimly imagined a hundred years ago. Many passages on alienation in the *Economic-Philosophical Manuscripts*, in the *German Ideology* and in the *Grundrisse* have only been truly realized in the last decades. And one could make the point that Marx's economic analysis of "pure capitalism" is much more a presentiment of what was going to happen during the 20th century than a description of what was happening under his eyes in the 19th century.

In any case, labor under neo-capitalism is more than ever alienated labor, forced labor, labor under command of a hierarchy which dictates to the worker what he has to produce and how he has to produce it. And this same hierarchy imposes upon him what to consume and when to consume it, what to think and when to think it, what to dream and when to dream it, giving alienation new and dreadful dimensions. It tries to alienate the worker even from his consciousness of being alienated, of being exploited.

Third, living labor remains more than ever the sole source of surplus value, the only source of profit, which is what makes the system tick. One can easily reveal the striking contradiction of a productive process heavily pregnant with unlimited potentials of making use-values abundant, but incapable of functioning smoothly and developing steadily because these use-values must first of all slip into the clothes of exchange-values, be sold and meet "effective demand" before they can be consumed. One can note the absurdity of a system in which science, technological progress, humanity's huge accumulated wealth of equipment, are the main basis for material production, but in which the "miserly appropriation of surplus labor" to use Marx's *Grundrisse* phrase, continues to be the only goal of economic growth: "Profit is our business, and business after all only means profit."

But all these contradictions and absurdities are real, living contradictions and absurdities of capitalism. These would attain their absolute limit in universal and total automation which, however, lies completely beyond its reach because living labor is indispensable for the further accumulation of capital. One has only to observe how the billion-dollar corporations haggle and shout like fishwives over a 50-cent wage increase here and two hours off the workweek there to see that, whatever ideologues and sociologists might argue, the hard facts of life confirm what Marx taught us: Capital's unlimited appetite for profit is an unlimited appetite for human surplus labor, for hours and minutes of unpaid labor. The shorter the workweek becomes, the higher the actual productivity of labor, the closer and more strictly do capitalists calculate surplus labor and haggle ever more furiously over seconds and fractions of seconds, as in time and motion studies.

Now precisely these three characteristics of modern labor — its key role in the productive process, its basic alienation, its economic exploitation — are the objective roots of its potential role as the main force to overthrow capitalism, the objective roots of its indicated revolutionary mission. Any attempt to transfer that role to other social layers who are unable to paralyze production at a stroke, who do not play a key role in the productive process, who are not the main source of profit and capital accumulation, takes us a decisive step backwards from scientific to utopian socialism, from socialism which grows out of the inner contradictions of capitalism to that immature view of socialism which was to be born from the moral indignation of men regardless of their place in social production.

Here we have to meet an objection often voiced both by so-called dogmatic Marxists and by avowed revisionists or opponents of Marxist theory. Haven't we given too general a definition of the working class under neo-capitalism? Shouldn't we restrict this category to the same group which came under this definition in the classical period of the socialist labor movement, to wit the manual workers actually engaged in production? Isn't it true that this category tends to decline, first relatively and then even in absolute figures, in the most advanced industrial countries of the West? Are not the mass of wage and salary earners to which we have constantly referred too vague and heterogeneous a grouping to be considered a social class in the Marxist sense of the word? And isn't the fading of the revolutionary potential of the working class in the Western metropolitan countries causally linked to this diminution of the manual production workers in the gainfully employed population?

The debate which inevitably arises from an answer to these questions could easily degenerate into a semantic squabble if the qualitative, structural nature of the proletariat is forgotten. Authors like Serge Mallet have correctly argued that the very nature of the productive process, under conditions of semi-automation or automation, tends to incorporate whole new layers into the working class. We do not accept Mallet's political conclusions, which have not at all been confirmed by the May revolt in France. In the forefront of that revolt we did not find only the "new" working class of highly skilled workers and technicians in semi-automated factories like those of the C. S. F. [General Electric] factory in Brest. Equally present were the classical conveyor-belt workers of Renault and Sud-Aviation and even the workers of some declining industrial branches like the shipyard workers of Nantes and Saint-Nazaire. The categories of the "old" and "new" working class created by Mallet do not correspond to the realities of the process.

But what is valid is the fact that the distinctions between the "purely" productive manual production worker, the "purely" unproductive clerical white-collar worker, and the "semi-productive" repairman become more and more effaced as a result of technological change and innovation itself, and that the productive process of today tends more and more to *integrate* manual and non-manual workers, conveyor-belt semi-skilled and data-processing semi-skilled, highly skilled repair and maintenance squads and highly skilled electronics experts. Both in the laboratories and research departments, before "actual" production starts, and in the dispatching and inventory departments, when "actual" production is over, productive labor is created if one accepts the definition of such labor given in Marx's *Capital.* For all this labor is indispensable for final consumption and is not simply waste induced by the special social structure of the economy (as for instance sales costs).

19

We can return to a point made before and state that just as the third industrial revolution, just as automation, tends to industrialize agriculture, distribution, the service industries and administration, just as it tends to universalize industry, so it tends to integrate a constantly growing part of the mass of wage and salary earners into an increasingly homogeneous proletariat.

This conclusion needs further elucidation. What are the indicators of the enhanced proletarian character of these "new" layers of workers which become progressively integrated into the working class?

We could cite offhand a series of striking facts: reduced wage differentials between white-collar and manual workers, which is a universal trend in the West; increased unionization and union militancy of these "new" layers, which is equally universal (in Brussels as in New York, schoolteachers, electricians, telephone and telegraph workers have been among the militant trade unionists in the last five years); rising similarities of consumption, of social status and environment of these layers; growing similarity of working conditions, i.e., growing similarity of monotonous, mechanized, uncreative, nerve-racking and stultifying work in factory, bank, bus, public administration, department stores and airplanes.

If we examine the long-term trend, there is no doubt that the basic process is one of growing homogeneity and not of growing heterogeneity of the proletariat. The difference in income, consumption and status between an unskilled laborer and a bank clerk or high-school teacher is today incommensurably smaller than it was fifty or a hundred years ago.

But there is an additional and striking feature of this process of integration of new layers into the working class under neo-capitalism: That is the equalization of the conditions of reproduction of labor-power, especially of skilled and semi-skilled labor-power. In the days of 19th century capitalism, there was elementary education for the manual worker, lower-middle-school education for the white-collar worker, high-school education for the technician; the reproduction of agricultural labor-power often didn't need any education whatsoever. Universities were strictly institutions for the capitalist class.

The very technological transformation, of which neo-capitalism is both a result and a motive force, has completely modified the levels of education. Today, outside of completely unskilled laborers for whom there are very few jobs any more in industry, strictly speaking, and for whom tomorrow there might be no jobs available in the whole economy, conditions of reproduction of skill for industrial workers, technicians, white-collar employees, service workers and clerks are completely identical in generalized high-school education. In fact, in several countries, radicals are fighting for compulsory education up to 18 years in a single type of school, with growing success.

Uniform conditions of reproduction of labor-power entail at one

20

and the same time a growing homogeneity of wages and salaries (value and price of labor-power), and a growing homogeneity of labor itself. In other words, the third industrial revolution is repeating in the whole society what the first industrial revolution achieved inside the factory system: a growing indifference towards the particular skill of labor, the emergence of generalized human labor, transferable from one factory to another, as a concrete social category (corresponding historically to the abstract general human labor which classical political economy found as the only source of exchange-value.)

Let it be said in passing that it would be hard to understand the dimensions and importance of the universal student revolt in the imperialist countries without taking into account the tendencies which we have sketched here: growing integration of intellectual labor into the productive process; growing standardization, uniformity and mechanization of intellectual labor; growing transformation of university graduates from independent professionals and capitalist entrepreneurs into salary earners appearing in a specialized labor market—the market for skilled intellectual labor where supply and demand make salaries fluctuate as they did on the manual labor market before unionization but fluctuate around an axis which is the reproduction cost of skilled intellectual labor. What do these trends mean but the growing proletarianization of intellectual labor, its tendency to become part and parcel of the working class?

Of course students are not yet workers. But it would be as wrong to define them by their social *origin* as it would be to define them by their social *future*. They are a social layer in transition. Contemporary universities are a huge melting pot into which flow youth of different social classes, to become for a certain time a new homogeneous social layer. Out of this interim layer there arises on the one hand an important part of the future capitalist class and its main agents among the higher middle classes, and on the other hand a growing proportion of the future working class.

But since the second category is numerically much more important than the first; and since the student milieu (precisely because of its transitional severance of basic bonds with a specific social class and because of its specific access to knowledge not yet excessively specialized) can gain a much sharper and much quicker consciousness than the individual worker of the basic ills of capitalist society; and since intellectual labor is increasingly a victim of the same basic alienation which characterizes all labor under capitalism, the student revolt can become a real vanguard revolt of the working class as a whole, triggering a powerful revolutionary upsurge as it did this May in France.

Let us restate the first conclusion we have arrived at. Neo-capitalism in the long run strengthens the working class much as did laissez-faire capitalism or monopoly capitalism in its first stage.

Historically, it makes the working class grow both numerically and in respect to its vital role in the economy. It thereby strengthens the latent power of the working class and underlines its potential capacity to overthrow capitalism and to reconstruct society on the basis of its own socialist ideal.

Immediately new questions arise. If this be so, will not the increased stability of the neo-capitalist system, its wide use of neo-Keynesian and macro-economic techniques, its avoidance of catastrophic economic depressions of the 1929-33 type, its capacity to shape the workers' consciousness through manipulation and the use of mass media, permanently repress these revolutionary potentialities? These questions boil down to two basic arguments which we shall deal with successively. One is the system's capacity to reduce economic fluctuations and contradictions sufficiently to assure enough reforms to guarantee a gradual easing of social tensions between capital and labor. The other is the system's capacity of integrating and engulfing the industrial proletariat as consumers and ideologically conditioned members of the society, to quote Baran and Sweezy's *Monopoly Capital*.

On the economic plane, we can briefly sketch the trends which make long-term "stability in growth" impossible for neo-capitalism. When the growth rate increases, as it did in Western Europe for 15 years from 1950 to 1965, then conditions of near-full employment enable the workers to rapidly increase real wages which, together with the rapidly increasing organic composition of capital, tend to push down the rate of profit. The system must react, and its reactions usually take two forms, or a combination of both. One is rationalization, automation, that is, increased competition between men and machines through reconstitution of the reserve army of labor to keep down the rate of increase of real wages. The other is voluntary or compulsory wage restraints, income policies, anti-strike and anti-union legislation, that is, attempts to prevent labor from utilizing relatively favorable conditions in the labor market in order to increase its share of the new value it creates.

Increased growth rates under neo-capitalist conditions of "administered prices," "investment through prices," state-guaranteed monopoly surplus profits and a permanent arms economy, also mean inflation.

Every attempt to stop inflation strangles the boom and precipitates a recession. Investment fluctuations and monetary disorders combine to increase economic instability, further abetted by stepped-up capital concentration both nationally and internationally, so that the system tends towards a marginal increase in unemployment and a generalized recession in the whole Western world. Both trends push down the rate of growth, as does the system's inability to constantly increase the rate of growth of armaments, that is, their share of the gross national product, without endangering enlarged reproduction, consequently economic growth itself. The accumulation of huge masses of surplus capital and of increasing surplus capacity in the capitalist world industry acts in the same sense of dampening the long-term rate of growth.

What emerges in the end is less the picture of a new type of capitalism successfully reducing overproduction than the picture of a temporary delay in the appearance of overproduction — *"zurueckstauen,"* as one says in German — by means of huge debt stockpiling and monetary inflation, which lead towards the crisis and collapse of the world monetary system.

Are these basic economic trends compatible with a secular decrease in social tensions between capital and labor? There is very little reason to believe this. Granted that the phases of rapid economic growth — more rapid in the last 20 years than in any comparable past period in the history of capitalism — create the material possibilities for increasing real wages and expanding mass consumption. But the attempts to base pessimistic predictions about the revolutionary potential of the working class on this trend of rising real wages overlooks the dual effect of the economic booms under capitalism on the working class.

On the one hand, a combination of near-full employment and a rapid rise of productive forces, especially under conditions of rapid technological change, likewise leads to an increase in the needs of the working class. That portion of the value of labor-power which Marx calls historically determined and is attributable to the given level of culture tends to increase most rapidly under such conditions, generally much more rapidly than wages. Paradoxically, it is precisely when wages rise that the gap between the value and the price of labor-power tends to grow, that the socially determined needs of the working class grow more rapidly than its purchasing power. The debate of the past decade in the United States and other imperialist countries on the growing gap between individual consumption and unsatisfied needs of social consumption, publicized by Galbraith as the contrast between private affluence and public squalor, illustrates this point.

Furthermore, rising real wages are constantly threatened by erosion. They are threatened by inflation. They are threatened by structural unemployment generated through technological change and automation. They are threatened by wage restraint and wage-freeze policies. They are threatened by recessions. The more the workers are accustomed to relatively high wages, the more they react against even marginal reductions in their accustomed level of consumption, the more all the just-named threats are potential starting points of real social explosion.

It is no accident that the working class youth is quicker to react and move to the forefront of these revolts. The older generations of workers tend to compare their miseries in the depression and during the war with the conditions of the last 15 years and can even view them as a state of bliss. Younger workers don't make these comparisons. They take for granted what the system has established as a social minimum standard of living, without being at all satisfied, either by the quantity or quality of what they get, and react sharply against any deterioration of conditions. That's why they have been in the front ranks of very militant strikes over the last two years in countries as widely different as Italy, West Germany, Britain and France. That's why they played a key role in the May revolution in France.

Even more important than the basic instability and insecurity of the proletarian condition which neo-capitalism hasn't overcome and cannot overcome is the inherent trend under neo-capitalism to push the class struggle to a higher plane. As long as the workers were hungry and their most immediate needs were unattended to, wage increases inevitably stood in the center of working class aspirations. As long as they were threatened by mass unemployment, reductions in the work-week were essentially seen as means of reducing the dangers of redundancy. But when employment is relatively high and wages are constantly rising, attention becomes gradually transferred to more basic aspects of capitalist exploitation.

The "wage drift" notwithstanding, industry-wide wage bargaining and attempts of neo-capitalist governments to impose incomes policies tend to focus attention more on the division of national income, on the great aggregates of wages, profits and taxes, than on the division of the newly created value at the factory level. Permanent inflation, constant debates around government fiscal and economic policies, sudden disturbances of the labor market through technological innovation and relocation of whole industries, draw the workers' attention in the same direction.

Classical capitalism educated the worker to struggle for higher wages and shorter working hours in his factory. Neo-capitalism educates the worker to challenge the division of national income and orientation of investment at the superior level of the economy as a whole.

Growing dissatisfaction with labor organization in the plant stimulates this very tendency. The higher the level of skill and education of the working class — and the third industrial revolution leaves no room for an uneducated and unskilled working class! — the more do workers suffer under the hierarchical and despotic work organization at the factory. The stronger the contradiction between the potential wealth which productive forces can create today and the immeasurable waste and absurdity which capitalist production and consumption implies, the more do workers tend to question not only the way a capitalist factory is organized but also what a capitalist factory produces. Recently, these trends found striking expression

24

not only during the May revolution in France, but also at the Fiat plant in Italy where the workers succeeded in preventing an increasing number of different types of high-priced cars from being manufactured.

The logic of all these trends puts the problem of workers' control in the center of the class struggle. Capitalists, bourgeois politicians and ideologues, and reformist Social Democrats understand this in their own way. That is why different schemes for "reform of the enterprises," for "co-management,""co-determination" and "participation" occupy the center of the stage in practically all Western European countries. When de Gaulle launched his "participation" demagogy, even the bonapartist dictatorship of Franco in Spain proclaimed that it was likewise in favor of working class participation in the management of plants. As for Mr. Wilson, he didn't wait a month to jump on the same bandwagon.

But parallel to these various schemes of mystification and deception is the growing awareness in working class circles that the problem of workers' control is the key "social question" under neo-capitalism. Questions of wages and shorter working hours are important; but what is much more important than problems of the distribution of income is to decide who should command the machines and who should determine investments, who should decide what to produce and how to produce it. British and Belgian trade unions have started to agitate these questions on a large scale; they have been debated in Italy at the factory level and by many left groupings. In West Germany, Sweden, Norway and Denmark they are increasingly subjects of debates in radical working class circles. And the May revolution in France was a clarion call for these ideas emanating from 10 million workers.

There remains the last objection. Have the monopolists and their agents unlimited powers of manipulating the ideology and consciousness of the working class, and can they not succeed in preventing revolt, especially successful revolt, notwithstanding growing socio-economic contradictions?

Marxists have recognized the possibility of "manipulation" for a long time. Marx wrote about the artificially induced needs and consumption of the workers a hundred and twenty-five years ago. Marxists have many times reiterated that the "ruling ideology of each society is the ideology of the ruling class." One of the key ideas of Lenin's *What Is to be Done?* is the recognition of the fact that, through their own individual effort and even through elementary class struggle on a purely economic and trade-union level, workers cannot free themselves from the influence of bourgeois and petty-bourgeois ideology.

The classical socialist labor movement tried to achieve such an ideological emancipation through a constant process of organization, education and self-action. But even during its heyday it didn't rally more than a minority fraction of the working class. And if one looks at the extremely modest proportions that Marxist education assumed in mass socialist parties like the German or Austrian Social Democracy before World War I (not to speak of the French CP before World War II), if one looks at the figures of subscribers to the theoretical magazines or students at study camps or workers' universities in those organizations, one can easily understand that even then they merely scratched the surface.

Of course things have become worse since the classical labor movement started to degenerate and stopped inoculating the working class vanguard in any consistent manner against the poison of bourgeois ideas. The dikes collapsed, and aided by modern mass media, bourgeois and petty-bourgeois ideology have penetrated deeply into broad layers of the working class, including those organized in mass Social-Democratic and Communist parties.

But one should guard against losing a sense of proportion in respect to this problem. After all, the working class movement arose in the 19th century under conditions where the mass of workers were far more dominated by the ideas of the ruling class than they are today. One has only to compare the hold of religion on workers in large parts of Europe, or the grip of nationalism on the French working class after the experience of the great French revolution, to understand that what looks like a new problem today is in reality as old as the working class itself.

In the last analysis the question boils down to this: Which force will turn out to be stronger in determining the worker's attitude to the society he lives in, the mystifying ideas he receives, yesterday in the church and today through TV, or the social reality he confronts and assimilates day after day through practical experience? For historical materialists, to pose the question this way is to answer it, although the struggle itself will say the last word.

Finally, one should add that, while "manipulation" of the workers' consciousness and dreams is apparently constant, so after all is the apparent stability of bourgeois society. It goes on living under "business as usual." But a social revolution is not a continuous or gradual process; it is certainly not "business as usual." It is precisely a sudden disruption of social continuity, a break with customs, habits and a traditional way of life.

The problems of the revolutionary potential of the working class cannot be answered by references to what goes on every day or even every year; revolutions do not erupt every day. The revolutionary potential of the working class can be denied only if one argues that the sparks of revolt which have been kindled in the working class mass through the experience of social injustice and social irrationality are smothered forever; if one argues that the patient and obstinate propaganda and education by revolutionary vanguard organizations cannot have a massive effect among the workers anywhere, anytime, whatever may be the turn of objective events. After all, it is enough that the flame is there to ignite a combustible mass once every 15 or 20 years for the system ultimately to collapse. That's what happened in Russia. That's what the May revolution in France has shown can happen in Western Europe too.

These epoch-making May events allow us to draw a balance sheet of long-term trends which confirm every proposition I have tried to defend here today. After 20 years of neo-capitalism, functioning under classical conditions, with a "planning board" which is cited as a model for all imperialist countries, with a state television system which has perfected a system of mass manipulation to uphold the ruling class and party, with a foreign policy accepted by a large majority of the masses, in May 1968 there were in France twice as many strikers as ever before in the history of the working class of that country; they used much more radical forms of struggle than in 1936, in 1944-46 or in 1955; they not only raised the slogan of workers' control, workers' management and workers' power more sharply than ever before, but started to put it in practice in a dozen big factories and several large towns. In the face of this experience it is hard to question the revolutionary potential of the working class under neo-capitalism any more. In the face of this experience it is hard to question the prediction that France, which is the politically classical country of bourgeois society, in the same way as Britain and the United States are its economically classical countries, is showing the whole Western world and not least the United States a preview of its own future. *De te fabula narratur!* [The story being told is about you!]

We have no time here to examine the interconnection between the workers' struggle for socialism in the Western metropolises and the liberation struggle of the colonial and semi-colonial countries as well as the struggle for socialist democracy in the countries of Central and Eastern Europe. These interconnections are manifold and obvious. There are also direct causal links between the upsurge of an independent revolutionary leadership in the Cuban and Latin American revolution, the heroic struggle of the Vietnamese people against U.S. imperialist aggression, and the emergence of a new youth vanguard in the West, which, at least in Western Europe, through the transmission belt of working class youth, has started to influence directly the development of the class struggle.

The main striking feature here has a more general and abstract character: the reemergence of active internationalism in the vanguard of the working class. The international concentration and centralization of capital, especially through the creation of the "multi-national corporation," gave capital an initial advantage over a working class movement hopelessly divided between national and sectional unions and parties. But now, in France, at one blow, the advanced workers

27

have cleaned the field of the rot accumulated over decades of confusion and defeat. They have cut through the underbrush of bourgeois nationalism and bourgeois Europeanism and have come out into the wide open space of international brotherhood.

The fraternal unity in strikes and demonstrations of Jewish and Arab, Portuguese and Spanish, Greek and Turkish, French and foreign workers, in a country which has probably been more plagued by xenophobia over the last 20 years than any other in Europe, triumphantly culminated in 60,000 demonstrators shouting before the Gare de Lyon: "We are all German Jews." Already a first echo has come from Jerusalem itself where Jewish students demonstrated with the slogan: "We are all Palestinian Arabs!" Never have we seen anything like this, on such a scale, and these initial manifestations warrant the greatest confidence in the world which will emerge when the working class, rejuvenated after two decades of slumber, will move to take power.

Most of you know that, both through political conviction and as a result of objective analysis of present world reality, I firmly believe that we are living in the age of permanent revolution. This revolution is inevitable because there is such a tremendous gap between what man could make of our world, with the power which science and technology have placed in his hands, and what he is making of it within the framework of a decaying, irrational social system. This revolution is imperative in order to close that gap and make this world a place in which all human beings, without distinction as to race, color or nationality, will receive the same care as the rulers today devote to space rockets and nuclear submarines.

What the socialist revolution is all about, in the last analysis, is faith in the unconquerable spirit of revolt against injustice and oppression and confidence in the ability of mankind to build a future for the human race. Coming from a continent which went through the nightmares of Hitler and Stalin, and emerged hardly a generation later holding high the banner of social revolution, of emancipation of labor, of workers' democracy, of proletarian internationalism, and witnessing in France more youth rallying around that banner than at any time since socialist ideas were born, I believe that faith is fully justified.

28

Ernest Mandel

REVOLUTIONARY STRATEGY IN THE IMPERIALIST COUNTRIES

Barred from entering the United States to deliver this talk, the author made a recording which was played at a conference entitled "Agencies of Social Change: Towards a Revolutionary Strategy for Advanced Industrial Countries," November 29, 1969.

Let me first say something about my exclusion. It demonstrates a lack of confidence on the part of the Nixon administration in the capacity of its supporters to combat Marxism on the battleground of ideas. I would not be carrying any high explosives, if I had come, but only, as I did before, my revolutionary views which are well known to the public.

Why should the Washington authorities be so afraid of my presenting them when many Marxist books are freely sold in the United States, including my own? In the nineteenth century the British ruling class, which was sure of itself, permitted Karl Marx to live as an exile in England for almost forty years. Times have certainly changed when the most powerful of capitalist governments today refuses a brief visit to an exponent of his doctrines!

On the other hand the press outcry and the protests over this action show that public opinion in the United States is very much alert to the dangers that threaten our basic freedoms.

A revolutionary strategy is possible only in a revolutionary epoch: this is a basic tenet of Marxism. A social revolution cannot be achieved until objective historical conditions have placed that revolution on the agenda. A social revolution cannot result simply from the desires, dreams, ideals of revolutionary-minded individuals. Its consummation requires a level of socio-economic contradictions which makes the overthrow of the ruling class objectively possible. And it needs the presence of another social class which, as a result of its place in the process of production, its weight in society, and its political potential, can successfully achieve this overthrow.

A revolutionary strategy in the advanced industrial countries today only makes sense, from a Marxist point of view, if one affirmatively answers these two questions: Is there a historical structural crisis of the world capitalist system? Does the working class have a revolutionary potential?

All those who consider that world capitalism has been a system in full expansion for twenty-five years or longer and remains so, that, in other words, the historical epoch of ascending capitalism is not yet over, cannot reasonably project a revolutionary strategy as a short- or medium-range perspective. They can, in the best of cases, maintain a principled opposition to the capitalist system on grounds similar to that of Western social democracy in its best period prior to World War I through a combination of the struggle for immediate reforms with general socialist propaganda. That's what the few reformists who call themselves Marxists in Europe—in the USA they seem to have disappeared—actually do.

There are also those who claim to be Marxists but assume that capitalism has gone through a period of tremendous worldwide expansion—Russia being capitalist, China being capitalist, and capitalism solving in one country after another the problem of socioeconomic underdevelopment. They, too, can remain consistent with their theoretical assumptions only by acting like reformists, i.e., by excluding any need for a revolutionary strategy as an immediate perspective in the West.

Revolutionary Marxists, on the other hand, have to prove that they are living in a historical epoch of crisis and disintegration of the world capitalist system, if they want to keep their search for a revolutionary strategy on the foundations of historical materialism. Evidence in that field is rather overwhelming. After all, nobody really believes that Presidents Johnson and Nixon have sent over half a million soldiers to Vietnam to prevent Ho Chi Minh from spreading capitalism to South Vietnam. What they want to stop is not capitalist competition by their competitors—who could seriously argue that the main economic competition which U.S. imperialism meets today on a world scale comes from North Vietnam or China, or even the Soviet Union at that!—but a challenge by an opposing social system, a challenge from anti-imperialist and anti-capitalist forces on a world scale. This challenge, which has existed ever since the October Revolution, is bigger today than it ever was, having spread to all six continents. Nothing of the kind existed in that epoch of expanding and triumphant capitalism which lasted through the nineteenth century up to World War I.

It is sometimes alleged that the growth of the productive forces in

Western imperialist countries since World War II — which is undeniable — disproves the existence of a historical crisis of decline and decomposition of world capitalism. This argument is not very convincing. It reflects a mechanistic conception of how a certain mode of production, how a certain set of relations of production, become fetters on a further development of the productive forces. A historical analogy will immediately clarify the point. Could one really argue that there was an absolute decline of the productive forces, say, in France during the fifty or twenty years prior to the Great French Revolution of 1789? Or, to take an even more striking example: Was the Russian Revolution of 1917 preceded by twenty years of stagnation and decline, or rather by twenty years of stormy expansion of the productive forces?

In his famous Preface to *A Contribution to a Critique of Political Economy*, written in January 1859, Marx specifies the necessary and sufficient preconditions for a historical epoch of social revolution in the most concise way possible: "At a certain stage of their development, the material forces of production in society come in conflict with the existing relations of production, or — what is but a legal expression for the same thing — with the property relations within which they have been at work before. From forms of development of the forces of production, these relations turn into their fetters. Then begins an epoch of social revolution."

The keystone of Marx's materialist theory of social revolution is therefore the concept of the *contradiction* between production and property relations on the one hand and the productive forces on the other hand. In today's world this conflict expresses itself in three ways. First, by the inability of world capitalism to solve any basic economic problems of the masses within the framework of the imperialist system. This is most graphically demonstrated by its inability to eliminate centuries-old backwardness in the so-called third-world countries. Second, by the growing inability of the system to contain the growth of productive forces — especially of the science-oriented third industrial revolution — within the framework of private property and the nation-state. Third, by a periodic large-scale revolt of masses of industrial and intellectual workers, as well as of youth in general, against the persistence of these capitalist relations of production, which mutilate their needs, their lives and their capacity for self-realization, and totally thwart the tremendous potential of human freedom and human self-realization opened up by contemporary industry, technology, and science.

Marx's famous prediction of a hundred years ago, that the productive forces would transform themselves more and more into destructive forces if they were not in time liberated from the fetters of private property and profit orientation, hits the nail squarely on the head. This does not imply an absolute decline in production but a much more frightful form of decay: a qualitative transformation of the results of increased output which threatens to destroy the last remnants of freedom of choice for the individual, the material biosphere of mankind, if not the very existence of the human race. The output of an ever-increasing mass of increasingly meaningless commodities of increasingly doubtful quality; the pollution of the atmosphere, land and water; and the threat of nuclear and biological warfare resulting from the growth of tremendous permanent war expenditures all testify to the realism of Marx's prediction.

If we approach the problem in this way, we will likewise have a key to judge the revolutionary potential of the working class. This is not primarily a question of gauging what workers *think*—going around with an electronic counter, measuring the number of workers reading capitalist or reformist newspapers and those reading revolutionary ones; comparing the affiliations to trade unions led by labor lieutenants of capitalism or to reformist working-class parties with the number of working-class members and sympathizers of revolutionary organizations, and then reaching the obvious conclusion that the overwhelming majority of the Western working class is not yet under the political influence or leadership of revolutionists. This is essentially a problem of analyzing the workers' force in reality and what they *do*, of ascertaining what the objective significance of their actions is.

In order to prove that the working class has lost its revolutionary potential, it would be necessary to prove that all the periodic explosions of working-class discontent—whose reality nobody can deny—are centered exclusively around problems of higher wages and shorter working hours, to enable them to have more time to consume capitalist commodities and enjoy the services of the capitalist leisure industries. But this image does not correspond to the reality of Western European workers' discontent; it does not correspond to the reality of the discontent of Japanese and Australian workers; it does not correspond to the reality of discontent in such an industrialized country of Latin America as Argentina; nor will it correspond to the future explosions of discontent in the United States since the politically advanced countries simply show the politically more backward one the image of its own future.

Any analysis of the May 1968 revolutionary upsurge in France cannot but arrive at the conclusion that its main thrust, on behalf of the working class, went far beyond questions of higher wages and shorter working hours. And since May 1968, we have had an uninterrupted series of examples reflecting this main thrust in all the main industrial countries of Western Europe: Italy, Britain, and even that supposed bulwark of conservatism and social conformism, Western Germany.

When workers challenge the basic organization of labor at plant level as they have done in many Italian factories (in one case, that of the Candy washing machine plant, even raising the problem of eliminating the basic division of labor between manual workers and white-collar employees by a job-rotation system); when they challenge the employers' right to lay off workers, close factories, or transfer equipment to other factories, as they are starting to do in Britain; when they raise at plant level the slogan of "Open the Books" in response to employers' refusal to grant demands, as they did during several recent wildcat strikes in Western Germany; when they seize and occupy a factory in answer to an employer's lockout, as they recently did at the Le Mans Renault plant in France, they thereby express their instinctive urge to raise the level of class struggle and of class confrontation from the elementary union level of the redistribution of income between profits and wages to the highest level prior to the struggle for power. This is the level of challenging Capital's right to dispose as it wills of workers and machines.

Such is the basic trend of the new working-class initiatives in Western Europe today. It is a clear challenge to the continuance of capitalist relations of production. This provides a striking illustration of the revolutionary potential of the working class. And this is why a revolutionary strategy in the Marxist sense of the word is both possible and indispensable, if the new upsurge of working class militancy which is now in full swing in Europe is not to end in defeat as it did in the previous three main periods of upsurge: that at the end of World War I; that during the mid-thirties; and that at the end of World War II.

To state that an analysis of the working class as an agency of social change should start from how the workers act and not from what they think does not at all imply that the question of their thinking — of their level of consciousness — is irrelevant to the processes of social change in the West. On the contrary: it is a basic thesis of Marxism that a socialist revolution, at least in an advanced industrial country, needs a high level of consciousness of the working class to be successful.

Socialism is the first social system in the history of mankind to be introduced by the conscious action of its collective creators and not, so to speak, behind the backs of the actors in history's drama. But once we understand that, in the last analysis, it is not consciousness which determines social existence, but social existence which determines social consciousness, it is in the realm of the conditions of production, of contradictions between human needs and capitalist relations of production, and of the inner contradictions of that capitalist mode of production itself that we have to discover the reasons for the dialectical development of working-class consciousness in its successive phases. Under normal conditions, the ruling ideology of society and the ruling pattern of behavior of workers cannot but be determined by the ideology, the values and patterns created and promoted by the ruling class. Then, under conditions of growing social crisis, a growing part of that same working class cannot but liberate itself progressively from that same ideology and pattern of behavior inspired by the ruling class.

Marcuse's main mistake is the assumption that, because the capitalist class can undoubtedly largely shape the consumer behavior and ideas of a majority of workers, it can thereby erase the acute awareness of alienation in the field of production. Alienation of the consumer and of the citizen is allegedly an efficient and sufficient means to suppress awareness of being alienated as producer. But this flies in the face of historical experience, of theoretical analysis, and simple common sense. After all, what a man does during his work; the frustrations he undergoes eight to ten hours a day — when one also counts the time spent going to and from the place of work — cannot but periodically influence his behavior at least as much, and very likely more than, the manipulated "satisfactions" he can "enjoy" four hours a day and during weekends.

It is true that a whole series of conjunctural factors is required to bring this reflection of the structural ills of capitalism to the threshold of the workers' consciousness. Conjunctural shifts in the trends of income and employment (a slight decrease of real wages after a long period of increases; a sudden increase in unemployment after a long period of full employment; a sudden threat of technological unemployment and mass layoffs in some key sector of industry, etc.); a crisis of leadership in the ruling class; a deep-going political crisis as a result of foreign imperialist adventures; a sudden upsurge of militancy and anti-capitalist activity in "marginal" sectors of society, like the students or the teachers: all these factors and many others can create a favorable climate for a growing awareness by the workers of their alienation as producers, and for a sudden shift of the class struggle to questioning the employer's authority in the shops, factories, and offices themselves. We are unlikely ever to find two large countries where an identical combination of circumstances will produce the general result we have described.

It is also true that purely spontaneous struggles challenging Capital's right and power to command men and machines cannot go beyond a certain level. We are here confronted with one of the most

34

complicated problems of Marxism and of sociology or contemporary history in general: the interaction between the spontaneous struggles of the workers, the role of the vanguard organizations, and the growth of working-class consciousness.

As a revolutionary Marxist, I do not believe that you can abolish an army or militarism by shortening guns millimeter by millimeter. Capitalism is a structure which can absorb and integrate many reforms (e.g., wage increases) and which automatically rejects all those reforms which run counter to the logic of the system (such as completely free public services which completely cover social needs). You can abolish the structure only by overthrowing it, not by reforming it out of existence.

But the understanding of the objectives of that revolutionary process, which can only take the form of social ownership of all the means of production and of conquering political power for the mass of the toiling people, must go hand in hand with an understanding of the dialectical unity between the struggle for reforms and the diffusion of revolutionary consciousness. Without the practical experience and partial victories acquired by the workers in their struggle for immediate demands — both economic and political ones — a rise of consciousness in the working class, a rise in its self-confidence, is impossible. And without such a rising self-confidence, the revolutionary insolence involved in challenging the rule of the most powerful, richest and best-armed ruling class which has ever existed on earth — the Western bourgeoisie — is just not imaginable.

The credibility of any plan for taking power, what Lenin called a revolutionary strategy, would in such cases be very low indeed in the eyes of broader masses. Gradual, molecular, nearly invisible processes of accumulating self-confidence, consciousness of the potential power of one's own class, are therefore of the utmost importance in preparing class explosions like May 1968 in France and the one which is now being prepared in Italy.

Objective contradictions in the system make periodic explosions of working-class discontent inevitable. But let me remind you of Lenin's statement that what distinguished a true revolutionist from a reformist was the fact that the former kept on spreading revolutionary propaganda even though the period was not — or not yet — revolutionary or prerevolutionary. Multiple skirmishes, together with continuous socialist revolutionary propaganda, prepare the working class for entering these explosions with a growing awareness of the need to challenge the system as a whole, of the need for a general struggle, a general strike, a challenge against the political as well as the social and economic power of the ruling class.

But this awareness in turn is not in itself sufficient. It does not guide

35

the working class to the next immediate step forward, once it has engaged in a general struggle. It does not answer the question: What do we do when we have occupied the factories? It is lack of consciousness of this decisive next step forward which again and again has stopped the working class in its tracks. This happened in the first years after World War I in Germany; in 1920 and 1948 in Italy; in 1936 and 1968 in France.

Two answers can be given to that question. The first one insists on the key role played by the building of a revolutionary party, which centralizes experience, consciousness, and assures its continuity. I shall come back to this question in a minute. It is obviously an essential part of the answer, but it is not the only one. Without a certain level of working-class consciousness and revolutionary self-activity, a revolutionary party cannot transform a struggle for immediate demands into a struggle challenging the very existence of the capitalist system. Even more so: without such a consciousness in at least part of the working class, such a revolutionary party cannot really become a mass party.

This is today the heart of the problem of revolutionary strategy in the Western industrialized countries. As I do not believe that capitalism will suddenly collapse as a result of its inner contradictions; as I do not believe that the main task of revolutionary socialists is just to sit on the sidelines and interpret current events, hoping for some miracle to bring about a revolution; as I firmly believe in the virtue of conscious intervention, in the key pedagogic role of struggle and experience drawn from struggle for the working class, my conclusion is the following: only by trying to expand actual living working-class struggles toward an incipient challenge against the authority of the employers, of the capitalist system, and of the bourgeois state inside the factories (and incidentally also in the neighborhoods, the living quarters of the working class) can a qualitative rise in working-class consciousness be achieved. This gives struggles for workers' control today in imperialist countries key strategic importance.

Through such struggles, and only through such struggles, can the workers achieve the understanding that what the overthrow of capitalism is all about in the last analysis is, to use Marx's famous formula, for the associated producers to take over the factories and the whole industrial system and run it for the common benefit of mankind, instead of having it run for accumulating profit and capital for a few giant financial groupings locked in deadly competition with each other. Through such struggles, and only through such struggles, can the workers build the actual organs through which they can, tomorrow, themselves take over the administration of the economy and the state: freely elected workers' committees at shop level, which will federate themselves afterwards locally, regionally, and internationally. That's what the conquest of power by the working class really means.

It is highly significant that one of the main demands born from the present upsurge in militancy of the Italian working class is the demand for free election of shop stewards at all levels of plant organization, including each conveyor belt, and the conception of these *delegati di reparto* as people who constantly challenge the chiefs, bosses, and foremen, the whole hierarchy which presses down on the worker in the capitalist plant. It is significant because in some giant factories, like the FIAT plant in Turin with 80,000 workers, the workers have already started to implement this demand even before they have conquered the "legal" right to do so. This is a historical step forward compared to the May 1968 revolt in France where, through an inability to set up organs of self-representation of this type, the workers were unable to prevent the Communist Party and union bureaucracy from reabsorbing their powerful upsurge through a combination of wage increases and new parliamentary elections.

A strategy of workers' control — a strategy of transitional demands, as they were called by the Communist International during its first years of existence, and later by Leon Trotsky and by the Fourth International — has, of course, many pitfalls. Any attempt by the workers to actually run a few factories isolated from the rest of the economy is doomed to failure, because they'll have to enter into competition with capitalist firms and submit to the inexorable imperatives of that competition. From this situation flow all the famous "laws of motion" of capitalism — as producers' cooperatives have found out again and again to their sorrow. But revolutionary socialists, while understanding all these pitfalls and dangers, will not be inhibited by them to the point of abstaining from attempts to broaden the class struggle through these challenges to capitalist authority. There is no other way to develop anti-capitalist consciousness among hundreds of thousands and millions of workers than along this road. Propaganda through the written or spoken word can convince individuals by the hundreds and, in the best of cases, by the thousands. Millions will be convinced only by action. And only by actions for transitional demands, for workers' control of production, which is the transitional demand *par excellence* in our epoch, will these millions see their understanding and consciousness rise to the level necessary for a revolutionary change in Western society.

To initiate, broaden, and generalize these experiences, you need a revolutionary vanguard organization. Without such an organization, isolated experiences or initiatives of groups of vanguard workers will remain just that: isolated experiences. The role of the centralization of consciousness, of generalization of experience, of continuous transmission of knowledge, as against the inevitably discontinuous character of mass struggles, can be played only by such a vanguard organization. Just as imperialism is a world system and the multinational corporation the most typical organizational unit of Capital today, so labor needs an international organization to realize that most difficult and most exalting of tasks: to derive a maximum of revolutionary understanding and consciousness from a maximum of worldwide revolutionary activity.

Individuals who adhere to a revolutionary vanguard organization can be motivated in the most variegated ways; they can come from very different social backgrounds. The impact which two decades of revolutionary upsurge of the peoples of Asia, Latin America, and Africa has had on the revival of revolutionary consciousness in the West has been incommensurably more important than the actual economic damage it has done to the functioning of the capitalist world system up to now. The impact which the revolutionary student movement, and revolutionary youth movement in general, has had upon a reawakening of the working class in Western Europe and Japan cannot be overestimated. Even in Western Germany, in the first wave of large-scale wildcat strikes for nearly forty years, one found thousands of essentially still unpolitical and unsocialist steelworkers in Dortmund imitating in their large demonstrations all the new forms of struggle introduced in Western German society by the revolutionary student movement during the previous two years.

But only if there exists a political leadership which can coordinate all these various forms of emergent revolutionary consciousness and direct them towards a central goal — the overthrow of capitalism, the conquest of political power — can the full momentum of the upsurge be maintained and the reawakened working class fully deploy its revolutionary potential. This of course includes a tremendous potential of spontaneous initiative. Actions by students and scientists; rent strikes and movements for women's liberation; revolts against disintegrating public services and uninhabitable cities; the taking over of hospitals and factories: all these multiple manifestations of revolt by all the creative layers of society against the capitalist relations of production, against oppression and exploitation in all their forms, can come into their own and avoid being co-opted by bourgeois society or ending in defeat only if they lead to a decisive showdown with the bourgeois class. In the last analysis, all these movements are political, because they pose the question of which class exercises power in society as a whole and in the state, and not merely the question: Who commands the machines in *one* plant? Who is to dictate the organization of *one* university? Who is to determine where *one* park should be located? Who is to run the buses in *one* city and in whose interest?

38

The unique unity of spontaneous mass revolt and mass organization in the full flowering of workers' democracy, on the one hand; and the concentrated consciousness, the distilled lessons of four centuries of modern revolutions and a hundred and fifty years of working-class struggles which is represented by a revolutionary party, on the other hand: this dialectical unity is embodied in the system of workers' councils which is the key answer to all the contemporary problems of mankind. For this system is a unique combination of free expression with dissent and unity of action, of liberty and efficiency, of individual self-expression and freely accepted collective solidarity. In such a system you can have, as you had in Russia in the first year of the revolution, ten, fifteen political tendencies coexisting and contending with one another for political hegemony, but at the same time bound together by a common concern to preserve and develop the revolution and fight against the common enemy. The inklings of a similar system became visible in the summer days of 1936 in Spain, when the workers with nearly naked hands broke the onslaught of the fascist army in practically every important industrial city of the country.

The inklings of a similar system are slowly emerging today in the revolutionary upsurge which has been maturing in Western Europe since May 1968 in France. It is history's answer to the central question of our epoch, whether freedom and democracy can flourish and coincide with the tremendous objective surge towards the national and international centralization of power initiated by contemporary technology. My answer is, yes, it can, in a system of democratically centralized and planned self-management of workers and toiling people.

This conclusion brings us back to the starting point. What are the agencies of social change in the West today? It is the basic thrust of the productive forces themselves, undermining, eroding, and shaking periodically in a violent way private property, the nation-state, and generalized market economy. It is the inevitable periodic explosions of labor's discontent against its alienation as producer, against the capitalist relations of production at plant level, locally, regionally, or nationally. It is the re-emergence of revolutionary consciousness in the youth through the transmission belts of the colonial revolution, the student revolt, the rise of a new generation of revolutionary teachers, scientists, technicians, and intellectuals. It is the potential fusion of that revolutionary consciousness with large masses of workers through campaigns and actions for transitional demands, culminating in workers' control of production. And it is the building of the revolutionary party and the revolutionary International. The better we succeed in combining all these elements, the closer we shall be to a socialist world and to the emancipation of labor and of all mankind!

George Novack

CAN AMERICAN WORKERS MAKE A SOCIALIST REVOLUTION?

This talk was delivered to the eighth national convention of the Young Socialist Alliance, held at the Chicago Circle Campus of the University of Illinois on November 28, 1968.

The capitalist rulers of the United States have choirs of troubadours, voluntary and hired, to chant their praises nowadays.

Intellectuals of all categories exalt their own functions in the fields of culture and communications.

Countless books, movies, and TV series depict the joys and cares of suburban middle-class families.

The press features the doings of youth, from the antics of hippies and yippies to the demonstrations of the campus rebels.

For a long time the Afro-American was, in the phrase of novelist Ralph Ellison, "the invisible man." But first the civil-rights movement and now the deeply felt black nationalist demands, exploding in ghetto uprisings, have pushed the black masses into view. Their grievances may be unsatisfied and their tactics deplored, but their forceful presence can no longer be ignored.

The least attention is being paid to the largest part of the American people. The white workers have almost fallen from public sight. Their social prestige is at the lowest point in this century. The wageworker has the fewest friends, admirers, and defenders among the intellectuals and in politically articulate circles. Who cares if the wealth-producers of the world's richest country have no Homer or even Walt Whitman to celebrate them?

The current devaluation of the social significance of the workers as a class, and the white workers in particular, stands in contrast with the latter half of the nineteen-thirties, when the mass production workers were invading the open-shop strongholds of big business and installing powerful unions in them. At that time they were widely believed to possess the potential energy, not only to change relations within industry, which they did, but to overthrow American capital-ism. This esteem for labor's progressive capacities persisted in radi-cal and even liberal quarters until after the postwar strike wave of 1945-46. (See *The New Men of Power*, written around that time by C. Wright Mills.)

In the two decades since, as a result of the prolonged prosperity, political reaction, union bureaucratism, and labor conservatism, the wageworking class has dropped to the bottom of the rating scale. Today there is "none so poor as to do them reverence." How point-less it seems to ask: Do the American workers have any revolution-ary potential? Can they break loose from established institutions, develop an anticapitalist consciousness, engage in a struggle for pow-er, and go on to build a socialist society?

Run through the hierarchy of American society and every level of it will come up with negative answers to these questions. The corpo-rate chiefs, their political agents, and the comfortable middle classes would agree that, except for a few disgruntled "subversives," the work-ers in the United States are content with their lot and station, have few deep grudges against the existing system, and will never look for-ward to changing it. Most professors and intellectuals look askance at the notion that ordinary workers have what it takes to organize them-selves and lead a mass movement that can challenge and displace the monopolist and militarist masters of their fate.

Skepticism about such qualifications among the workers extends beyond the well-to-do. The union bureaucrats, who do not permit the ranks to lead their own unions, hardly expect them to run the whole of American society. Afro-Americans view privileged and prejudiced white workers as indifferent and hostile to black emancipation, and they are to a certain extent correct.

In their quest for forces that can bring about revolutionary change in the contemporary world, some young radicals look toward the "poor," the unemployed, the lumpenproletariat, student rebels, and the peoples of the Third World. They turn in every direction but one: the millions of industrial workers in their own land. Although the Social-ist and Communist parties preserve some ritual rhetoric, inherited from their Marxist pretensions, that links the prospects of socialism with the working class, in practical politics they display a lack of faith in its independent power by supporting capitalist parties and liberal politicians and refusing to propagandize for a labor party based on the unions.

This attitude has been formulated in philosophical terms by Prof. Herbert Marcuse in his popular book, *One-Dimensional Man*. In a symposium at the University of Notre Dame in April 1966, he ar-gued that Marxism has broken down in its central contention that the working class is the predestined gravedigger of capitalism. "In the advanced industrial countries where the transition to socialism was to take place, and precisely in those countries, the laboring classes are

41

in no sense a revolutionary potential," he asserted. More recently, in an interview published in the October 28, 1968, *New York Times*, Marcuse flatly ruled out any possibility of revolution in the United States. Revolution is inconceivable without the working class and that class is integrated in the affluent society and "shares in large measure the needs and aspirations of the dominant classes," he stated.

In a reassessment of Marx's theory of the revolutionary role of the industrial proletariat at the 1967 Socialist Scholars Conference in New York, *Monthly Review* editor Paul Sweezy propounded the proposition that, in sharp contrast with the peasant masses in the Third World, the advances of modern technology and its prodigious productivity in a developed democratic capitalist framework tend to shape a proletariat which is less and less revolutionary.

These write-offs of the workers by the Left have been matched by liberals who proceed on non-Marxist premises. Thus, after announcing that Marx erred in expecting the working class to be the prime agency of revolutionary change, David Bazelon in *Power in America: The Problem of the New Class* assigns that function to the managers and technocratic intellectuals who he thinks are about to supplant the capitalists as the future ruling class.

To round out this record of disparagement, most American workers would hardly give positive answers to a pollster who asked whether they had the need, right, or prospect of taking control of the economic and political system from the present possessors of power and property.

Hardly anyone but revolutionary Marxists nowadays retains faith in the anticapitalist strivings and sentiments of the working people or believe that they can in time participate in a mighty movement oriented toward socialist objectives. For adhering to these convictions and being guided by them, we are looked upon as ideological freaks and political fossils, ridiculous relics of a bygone era, dogmatists who cling to outworn views and cannot understand what is going on in front of our own eyes.

Indeed, it may seem quixotic to put up countervailing arguments against such an overwhelming preponderance of public opinion and dulled class consciousness among the workers themselves. Why not go along with the crowd?

Unfashionable as it may be, Marxists have substantial reasons for their adamant resistance on this point. Their convictions are not an affirmation of religious-like faith. They are derived from a scientific conception of the course and motor forces of world history, a reasoned analysis of the decisive trends of our time, and an understanding of the mainsprings and the necessities of capitalist development. Marxism has clarified many perplexing problems in philosophy, sociology, history, economics, and politics. Its supreme achievement is the explanation it offers of the key role of the working class in history.

This is far too serious an issue to be treated in an offhand way.

Nothing less is at stake than the destiny of American civilization and with it the future of mankind.

So grave a question cannot be definitively disposed of by reference to the present mood, mentality, and lack of political organization of the workers themselves. Nor can it be permanently suppressed. It keeps reasserting itself at each new turn of events. No sooner has the revolutionism of the working class been dismissed for the hundredth time than it returns from exile to haunt its banishers.

The year 1967, for example, marked the fiftieth anniversary of the October revolution, when the workers did conquer power for the first time in history, opening a breach in the structure of world capitalism which has been widened and deepened by a series of subsequent socialist revolutions. Will this process never be extended to the United States when it has already come within ninety miles of its shores?

The general strike of ten million French workers in May-June 1968 disclosed an unsuspected readiness for anticapitalist action in the advanced industrial West. Cannot the American workers become imbued at some point with a similar militancy?

There is another side to this problem. Those who deny any latent radicalism in the industrial workers seldom appreciate what consequences logically flow from this negative position in the areas of most concern to them.

If the working masses cannot be counted on to dislodge the capitalists, who else within the country can do that job? It would be exceedingly difficult to point out another social force or find a combination of components that could effectively act as a surrogate for the industrial workers. The struggle against capitalist domination then looms as a lost cause and socialist America becomes a Utopia.

Recognition of this difficulty gives rise to pessimistic forecasts of America's future. Some see the iron heel of fascism already poised above the nation; others emphasize the powerlessness of the Left. People who seriously envisage such a perspective must logically reconcile themselves to the eventual unloosing of a nuclear holocaust by the American imperialists at bay.

A typical instance of such prostration was provided by the historian Gabriel Kolko of the University of Pennsylvania in an article on "The Decline of American Radicalism in the Twentieth Century," published in the September-October 1966 issue of the now defunct *Studies on the Left.* After pronouncing Marxism obsolescent, he concluded: "Given the consensual basis of American politics and society in the 20th century, and the will of the beneficiaries of consensus to apply sufficient force and power at home and abroad when resistance to consensus and its hegemony arises, the new left must confront the prospect of failure as an option for radical, democratic politics in America. Rational hopes for the 20th century now rest outside America and in spite of it. . . ."

In view of the omnipotence of the ruling class and the weakness of its internal opposition, all that radicals can do is "to define a new intellectual creed at home which permits honest men to save their consciences and integrity even when they cannot save or transform politics." As though to verify these arguments, *Studies on the Left* shut up shop shortly thereafter, and its editors have scattered in search of a new critique of "post-industrial society" to save (or should we say "salve") their scholarly consciences.

Before succumbing to such sentiments of hopelessness, it would seem advisable at least to reexamine the problem in a more rounded way. It might then be seen that the Marxist analysis and inferences on the prospects of the American working class are not so unfounded as the critics make out.

The present situation of American labor

The potential of any class is derived from the place it occupies in the dynamics of economic development. Is it advancing or receding, rising or declining in the system of production? From all statistical indices it is plain that the small family farmer falls into the second category. Is the industrial worker shriveling as well?

All over the world — regardless of the social form of production — industrialization and urbanization is causing the proletariat to grow in size and gain in economic, social, and political importance. The wage-working class, defined as those who sell their own labor power to the owners of capital, is no exception to that rule in the most advanced of all the industrial countries. Between 1880 and 1957 the ratio of wage earners of all sorts in the gainfully employed population of the United States rose steadily from 62 percent to 84 percent, with a corresponding decline for entrepreneurs of all kinds (from 37 percent to 14 percent).

The number of jobs in American industry has more than doubled since 1940, rising from 33 to well over 70 million. This army of wage earners operates the most complex and up-to-date productive facilities and produces the most abundant and diversified output of goods. The product of their energies and skills provides the riches of the owners of industry and supports their gigantic armed forces.

Thanks to the prodigious capacities of the productive apparatus, this working class has the highest wage rates and living standards, even though it receives a diminishing share of the annual wealth it creates. Eighteen millions or so have organized strong unions and engaged in many of the biggest and bitterest strikes in labor's history.

At the same time most members of this class are extremely retarded in political and social outlook, the least aware of their class status and responsibilities, racist-minded, privileged, and conservatized. They remain the only working class of the highly industrialized countries which has not cut loose from subservience to the capitalist parties and established a mass political organization of their own, whether of a Laborite, Socialist, or Communist type. Although they may be steady union-dues payers, they are by and large uneducated in Marxist ideas and the socialist program.

Many of today's young radicals are far more impressed by the undeniable shortcomings of the labor movement than by any of its positive accomplishments. Sometimes they appear to deny it any progressive features. They slight the significance of the sheer existence of powerful union organizations which act as a shield against lowering wages and working conditions and check the aggressions of capitalist reaction. They leave out of consideration the working conditions of a century ago, before unionization: the fourteen- to sixteen-hour day, the exploitation of child labor, the early mortality rate for all workers; and they neglect to study what happens when unions are exceptionally weak and fragmented — or destroyed — in the epoch of imperialism, for instance in Mussolini's Italy or Hitler's Germany.

According to the anti-Marxist ideologues, whatever else happens, the workers will never become a force ready, willing, and able to transform the United States. Their ranks are so smugly and snugly integrated into the mass "consumer society" that they can have no compelling reasons to turn against it. It is out of the question for them to attain the political or ideological level of their European counterparts and certainly not the revolutionary temper of the Cuban workers.

Such a long-term prognosis rests upon two suppositions. One, that American capitalism has been immunized against severe crises and will maintain its domestic stability indefinitely. Two, that the present characteristics, attitudes, and relations of the working force are essentially unalterable by any foreseeable change in circumstances. Much hinges then on the prospects of U. S. monopoly capitalism in the last third of the twentieth century. What are these likely to be?

The outlook for American capitalism

Despite the elimination of private property elsewhere, the capitalist rulers of America today have an arrogant faith in the longevity of their system. They firmly believe that the empire of the almighty dollar is assured of perpetual dominion at home and abroad.

From an offhand glance at developments since the Civil War, the case for their continued supremacy would appear unassailable. Over the past century the magnates of capital have succeeded in concentrating economic, political, military, and cultural power in their hands. They have emerged from two world wars stronger and richer than before. They hold the commanding heights within the country and over two-thirds of the globe.

While peoples on other continents have become more and more cognizant of the revolutionary nature of our epoch, Americans consider themselves completely detached from it because of the contradictory effects the international upheavals since 1917 have had on the fortunes of American capitalism.

While the system that it is committed to defend to the death has been losing ground step by step to the socialist forces on a world scale, U. S. capitalism has been gaining enormously at the expense of its rivals. Today it towers above them all.

This country has been the prime capitalist beneficiary of the cataclysmic changes that have marked the first period of the transition from capitalism to socialism. The main beneficiary of the capitalist past, it has flourished more than ever during the first phase of capitalism's decline. As it holds the fort for the rest of the capitalist camp, the United States has drawn into itself most of the residual vitality of the disintegrating capitalist order.

This temporarily favorable aspect of the world situation for America's ruling class accounts for the unexampled strength of monopolist domination, the stability of its social alignments, the complacency of its political outlook. The eminence that so pleases the rich and the very rich and deludes the rest of the American people is viewed as a fitting culmination and reward of the entire career of American civilization.

The basic reasons for the political backwardness which appears so insuperable and everlasting are not to be found in any irremovable psychology of the American people and its working class but rather in the exceptionally auspicious circumstances of the development of American bourgeois society. It was the offspring of a lusty young capitalism which swept everything before it from the time the New World was opened up for settlement and exploitation half a millennium ago.

The population of the United States has been the most favored, pampered, and even spoiled child in the family of capitalist nations. Capitalism has attained the most luxuriant growth here in almost every respect. This consummate development of capitalism, which is the outstanding peculiarity of our history, has set its stamp upon the thinking, values, and outlook of almost every American. That is why the worship of the golden calf, the frantic chase after the fast and not so elusive buck, and confidence in the eternity of this system are so deeprooted and widespread. Any suggestion that world capitalism in general, and its American segment in particular, has reached its zenith seems incredible to the ordinary citizen who expects that the system as he knows it will, like old man river, just keep rolling along.

These devout believers in the perpetuity of U. S. capitalism fail to take into consideration the impact of five mighty tendencies upon its further development.

First is the fact that America's wealth and preponderance have been gained, and are being sustained, at the expense of the poverty and weakness of less fortunate countries in other parts of the world. Their

46

blood and flesh fatten the vulture of imperialism. The gap between rich and poor keeps widening on a global scale. American citizens make up one-fifteenth of the world's population and consume one-half of its total output.

Second, this unequal and oppressive relationship has its consequences. Those underdeveloped — or, more accurately, overexploited — countries which have been shut off from almost all the benefits of capitalist expansion, while suffering from imperialist depredation and domination, are increasingly resorting to anticapitalist actions to achieve their liberation. They are determined to get access to a rightful share of the conquests of modern civilization. This is the motivation and meaning of the irrepressible revolutionary movements in Asia, the Near East, Africa, and Latin America.

Third, the predominant trend of history since 1917 has not been the building up but the breaking down of world capitalism. This process of socialist expansion has already established workers' states all the way from the Adriatic in Europe to the Pacific Ocean; in Cuba it has come within hailing distance of the United States. This international anticapitalist struggle, which is the ascending social and political trend of the twentieth century, celebrated the first half-century of its conquests in October 1967. The next half-century does not promise fewer advances toward socialism than the first.

Fourth, the spread of world revolution has already administered stiff jolts to American imperialism and continually confronts its strategists with grave problems on the foreign field. Their disastrous setback in Vietnam is only a down payment on the enormous costs they must incur in undertaking the overambitious design of policing the world for the preservation of the profiteering way of life.

Finally, the cumulative effects of all the problems growing out of the convulsions of a chronically sick capitalism are sooner or later bound to have sizable and serious repercussions within the United States itself. They will tend to undermine its stability, upset its conservatism, and give rise to new forms of mass radicalism. These have already announced themselves in the strivings of black America for national self-determination, the disaffection among the youth, and the antiwar movement that changed the face of American politics in 1968.

It should be noted that these expressions of discontent emerged amidst the longest boom of the twentieth century and virtually full employment. A slump in economic activity would intensify the growing dissidence in the unions and add a sizable amount of labor unrest to the array of opposition to the monopolist regime.

Is it reasonable to expect that the United States alone will remain indefinitely separated from the world historical movement toward socialism when it is already up to its ears in every other international development? It is more likely that its reckless and far-ranging activities in attempting to safeguard its system from decline and destruction, combined with the fluctuations in its economy, will bring about an eventual radicalization of its own working class.

Japanese seismologists monitor micro-earthquakes every day to detect signs of impending tremors that portend major upheavals. So the recurrent strikes at the lowest ebb of the class struggle in the United States serve as reminders that its workers cannot be completely counted out as a factor in the calculations of American radicalism.

Possible precipitants of labor radicalism

The skeptics who repose unlimited confidence in the longevity of capitalism rule out the possibility that the workers will be any more insurgent in the next twenty years than the last. What will incite them to change from being a prop to a peril to capitalism, they ask. Won't they become more and more like the housebroken "cheerful idiots" depicted by C. Wright Mills?

Surprisingly, it may turn out that the past two decades of inertia were not a totally dead loss. They may have enabled the working class to rejuvenate its ranks and accumulate energies which await a suitable occasion for discharge. Thus the French workers, who appeared to be disarmed under de Gaulle, seized the tenth anniversary of his assumption of authoritarian power to launch the greatest of all general strikes and make an aborted bid for power.

The United States has hardly been a model of social peace since Johnson started bombing North Vietnam in 1965 — and the rising tide of radicalism is far from its crest. The workers will not join it solely as a result of verbal exhortations. But they can get moving again in reaction to some whiplash of the capitalist regime. Here the subsequent course of international economic development will be the decisive factor.

Throughout the postwar expansion the exceptionally high productivity of the American economy has enabled its capitalists to dominate the world market despite the higher wage scale of our industrial workers. Now the unbeatable international advantages enjoyed by U.S. corporations for two decades are fast diminishing as other industrialized countries have reequipped, rationalized, and modernized their productive systems. Although West European and Japanese industries continue to trail behind the American giants in the computer and aircraft fields, they are today fully capable of challenging them in auto, steel, chemicals, shipbuilding, and many lines of consumer goods.

Under intensified foreign competition, U.S. corporations will be increasingly pressed to shave their costs, beginning with the cost of labor. The average wage of the American worker has been two and a half times that of the West European and five times greater than the Japanese. Big business will have to try to reduce this immense wage differential through direct or indirect moves against the earnings and living standards of the industrial work force. As the unions engage in defensive actions against such attacks, sharp tension can quickly replace the prevailing toleration between the bosses and the workers.

The resurgence of labor radicalism may come from the flagging of the long-term postwar capitalist expansion and an extended downturn in the industrial cycle — or it may be precipitated by intensified inflation. It could be provoked by anger against antilabor legislation or by resistance to another military venture and debacle of U. S. imperialism. It could be hastened by the impact of a black insurrection, student clashes with the authorities, as in France, or by the penetration of these forces into the unions through black caucuses and radicalized young workers. The possibilities are so diverse that it is impossible to foretell where or how the break in the dike will come.

The irregular development of American radicalism from 1928 to 1968

The widespread underrating of the working class comes from reliance on short-range criteria. Marxism has other standards of judgment. Its general strategy in the struggle for socialism is based upon a long-term, many-sided and dialectical approach to the development of the proletariat.

It is important to note that from 1928 to 1968 the struggles of the three main anticapitalist elements have unfolded in a disparate manner and at an uneven tempo. The industrial workers, the black masses, and the students have manifested fluctuating degrees of radicalism over those forty years which have brought them into differing relations with one another as well as with the ruling class.

The American workers of the nineteen-twenties were far more passive, helpless, and poorly organized than today. Many experts at that time could not figure out how these weaknesses might be overcome, and it was not easy to do so. The touchstone of labor's impotence in their eyes was its inability to introduce unionism into basic industry where most low-paid workers were located.

They marshaled imposing reasons why the workers were unlikely to emerge from disorganization. The workers were divided against themselves: native against foreign-born, white against black, craft workers against mass production workers. The anti-union forces were rich, crafty, and powerful. The magnates of capital had the workers at their mercy. They controlled the courts, legislatures, Congress, and the press. They used the blacklist, their private police, labor spies, and reserves of strikebreakers to crush and victimize organizers in the shops.

Moreover, the AFL officialdom was uninterested in bringing unionism to the unorganized. How, then, were the mass production workers to organize themselves? They were considered too unintelligent and unaware of their own interest and bereft of the necessary resources, national connections, and experience.

The most telling argument advanced by the empiricists was the failure of every effort that militants and radicals had made for forty years to organize basic industry. The campaigns undertaken by Eugene Debs in the early eighteen-nineties; by the De Leonists, Wobblies, and left Socialists before the first world war; and, finally, by the Communists in the nineteen-twenties had all come to nothing.

The gloomy prognosis drawn from these empirical facts had one flaw: it assumed that previous conditions would prevail with undiminished effect from one decade to the next. However, the 1929 crash intervened and upset many things. Once the workers recovered from the paralyzing onset of the depression, and industry picked up in 1933, their morale and fighting spirit revived with it. Before the end of the decade, they broke down the open shop and unionized basic industry.

Such swings tell a great deal about the mutability in the disposition of social forces. Consider the contrasting positions of the white workers and the black people in the nineteen-thirties and the nineteen-sixties. This is as instructive as the reversals that took place in the state of the working class from the nineteen-twenties to the nineteen-thirties and from the thirties to the sixties.

Labor was on the offensive against corporate capital in the nineteen-thirties, with the white workers in the lead. Once the black workers became convinced that they were really welcome in the new industrial unions, they joined wholeheartedly with the white workers in the organizing struggles of the CIO. In fact, pro-union sentiment was stronger in the black community as a whole than in the white community in the late thirties and early forties.

Black militancy and black radicalism were expressed mainly through general labor struggles in the thirties, rather than as a specifically black movement. There were scattered pockets of black nationalist organization, and black nationalist sentiment was undoubtedly more widespread than most whites realized, but the strength and potential of Afro-Americans as an autonomous force had not yet been expressed in any significant organizational form. It was not until 1941, with the emergence of the short-lived March on Washington movement, that there appeared the first signs of a nationwide nationalist awakening, or reawakening, since the heyday of Garveyism in the nineteen-twenties. Its development was slow and erratic during the forties and early fifties, but by the sixties it had become one of the central features of the present epoch.

So the relative roles of the white workers and the black people became reversed. While the white workers were by and large quiescent, millions of black Americans were now pounding against the status quo. The initiative in struggle, held by the working class in the nineteen-thirties, had now passed into the hands of blacks as a people.

Suppose that learned sociologists, projecting from the state of affairs in the thirties, had concluded that the black people never would or could rise up on their own and take the lead in social protest. Would such an extrapolation be better grounded than the current presumption that apathetic white workers, now in the rearguard, must be disqualified as a fighting force for the rest of the century, or even the coming decade?

What about students? Throughout the nineteen-thirties they played a small part in the surge of radicalism dominated by labor. During the great strike wave from 1945 to 1947 they were not heard from. At that point could they not have been written off for all time as a ferment for revolution? Indeed, they remained "the silent generation" through the nineteen-fifties and did not pass over to radicalism until they were animated by the civil-rights movement, the Cuban Revolution, and the anti-H bomb demonstrations in the early sixties.

Such pronounced irregularities in the radical activities of diverse sectors of society speak against making hasty categorical judgments about their respective capacities for combat from their postures over a limited time. The prophets of gloom may easily mistake the recharging of the energies of the American working class for their exhaustion.

Proposed alternatives to the working class

Once the workers have been canceled out as the chief bearer of social progress, the question is insistently posed, Who will take their place? Obviously, the peasantry, which has been the most massive revolutionary battering ram in the colonial countries, cannot serve as a substitute in the United States.

One answer is that the twenty-two million Afro-Americans will fill the vacancy because they occupy a comparable status as an oppressed colonial people inside the imperialist monster. At the present stage the battlers for black liberation unquestionably stand in the front line against the capitalist power structure. They have not waited for anyone else to launch a vigorous attack upon the caste system that victimizes them in so many ways. And they have begun to form their own leadership and create their own organizations in pursuing that struggle.

However, these facts do not exhaust the problem of their place in the overall development of the American revolution. Black Americans have need of powerful allies at home as well as abroad in order to overcome "the man" and win liberation from the oppression of Uncle "Sham." They can count on sympathetic support from radical students and intellectuals. But that is hardly enough. Remote and improbable

51

as it seems in the prevailing situation, the principal source of internal reinforcement for their liberation movement can come only from the white end of the labor force.

The long-term strategical formula for throwing off the rule of the rich is an anticapitalist alliance in action between insurgent Afro-Americans and militant white industrial workers. No other coalition of forces can carry through that task. Like the workers and peasants in colonial lands, the two will triumph together or not at all.

Some non-Marxists rebut this strategical orientation by counterposing the aggressiveness of black America to the docility of the white workers. They thereby lose sight of significant similarities in the socio-economic positions of the two parts of the proletariat which can acquire great importance at a later time.

The black liberation movement itself has a dual character. It combines the democratic struggle for self-determination of a national minority with a drive for proletarian demands and objectives. This is because the black masses are not peasants in the countryside who aspire to change agrarian relations. They are largely wageworkers penned in city slums who are up in arms against intolerable conditions of life and labor.

In 1957-58, for example, almost 90 percent of the half-million blacks in Detroit were blue-collar workers. Most were in the auto, steel, and chemical plants and belonged to the industrial unions. Many participated in the 1967 uprising. According to John C. Leggett's study, *Class, Race and Labor* (1968), they are not only highly race conscious but "more class conscious than whites." That is, they are more outraged by the privations imposed on them by "the big-money class" and readier to resist it. The same holds true for Chicago and other centers of industry, as the black caucuses springing up in unions from the East to the West Coast indicate.

The composite character of the superexploited wage slaves in the cities makes their struggles doubly explosive. The democratic demands of the black people for an end to discriminatory treatment and racism are fused with their proletarian demands for jobs, rank-and-file control of the unions, more welfare, and other essentials. Although many nationalist black militants do not yet see the matter in this light, they act as the anticapitalist vanguard of the entire American working class.

However much the black masses are now estranged from the white workers, both are objectively yoked together through their joint subordination to the profiteers. They constitute two distinct segments of a single labor force. They are, to be sure, diametrically different in certain respects, since black and white are unequally subjected to the pressures of capitalist exploitation. Nevertheless, their common economic positions vis-a-vis the ruling economic and political power tend to draw them closer together, despite the width of their divergences.

Apart from the national minorities or along with them, anarchistically inclined thinkers imagine that such elements as the chronically unemployed, the lumpenproletariat, the hippies or other temporary dropouts from bourgeois society can be alternative gravediggers of capitalism. But they cannot explain how these outcast groupings can organize themselves or others for sustained economic or political activity of any kind, whatever spasmodic and despairing outbursts they may indulge in.

C. Wright Mills looked to the dissidents among the "intellectual apparatus" as "a possible immediate, radical agency of change." The wageworkers, he theorized, acted as a decisive political force only in the early stages of industrialization. Now these workers had become coopted into the bureaucratized "mass consumption" United States and the "cultural workers" would have to lead the struggle against "the power elite."

The general experience of the past decade has not confirmed this conclusion of the empirical sociologist, or rather, it has certified its limitations. Dissident intellectuals can play significant roles in starting and stimulating oppositional currents against authoritarian regimes and unpopular policies, as Czechoslovakia in the East and the anti-Vietnam-war teach-ins in the West have indicated. But however great their political impact, nowhere have their initiatives or activities in and of themselves overturned an established social or political regime and put a new one in its place.

Students have likewise demonstrated the world over that they can play a vanguard role in opposing official and unofficial reaction and detonating struggles of broader scope by setting an example of resistance for other forces to imitate. But in the dynamics of the revolutionary process as a whole, their intervention is auxiliary to the decisive power of the working masses. Once the ten million French strikers returned to work in June 1968, the student rebels, who had touched off the workers' offensive, could not sustain their confrontation with the de Gaulle government.

The perspectives of a triumphant fight to the finish against capitalist domination and imperialism are inseparably connected with the entry of the workers onto the arena. Who else can organize and mobilize a counterpower strong enough to challenge and crush the powers-that-be? Who else is in a position to take control of the means of production, socialize them, and plan their operation? Who else can become the directors of the new social order? To understand this and act upon it distinguishes the vanguard students who become Bolsheviks from all others.

There is a further consideration. The non-Marxist rebels want greater democracy. Yet, paradoxically, the repudiation of the workers as the central agency of social reconstruction leads to extremely undemocratic options.

The white and black workers and their families compose the vast majority of the American people. Suppose some other agency is delegated or destined to lead the way to the abolition of capitalism. What relation is the savior-force to have to the working masses during this process? If the workers are not self-active, it could at best be paternalistic. In that event, the revolutionary movement would fall under the auspices of a benevolent elite or a maleficent bureaucracy.

How does such a mode of development square with the insistence of these young rebels that they are more devoted to democratic methods than the Marxists and opposed to all forms of elitism or bureaucratism? How are they, or anyone else, going to promote a revolution along democratic lines without the conscious consent and active participation of the wageworking majority? And what happens if that majority remains antipathetic and resistant to the ongoing revolution — as they should, according to certain preconceptions? If the workers cannot be revolutionized under any conceivable circumstances, then the prospects for expanding American democracy are no brighter than those for achieving socialism.

Depreciating the working class

It is ironical that young rebels who reject conformism to big business mimic its low opinion of the working class. One reason for this attitude is a limited historical vision. Contemporary Americans are divided, according to University of Michigan sociologists, into the "depression" and the "prosperity" generations.

The new radicals belong to the latter group. Cradled in the prosperity and domestic stability of the postwar Western world, they are acquainted only with a nonmobilized union movement. They have never witnessed combative legions of labor at first hand nor seen what they can accomplish. They regard the union structure as an unbreakable solid block and make no distinction between the membership and the officialdom that sits upon it. Consequently, they feel as alienated from the ranks of labor as the ranks do from them.

Many unwittingly share the disdain of middle-class intellectuals for less formally educated people. They visualize the mass of workers as contented cattle who cannot look beyond their bellies or ever be inspired by a call to struggle for broad social causes and political aims.

Although they may have taken courses in economics or sociology, they fail to perceive how the psychology of the better-paid workers has been debased by middle-class values. The worst aspect is not, as some think, an artificially stimulated craving for meretricious goods and the latest gadgets.

Far more vicious and pernicious are the feelings of inferiority induced in the popular masses through systematic indoctrination in the standards of the master class which underrate their real worth to

54

society. The self-reliance of the workers is so weakened that they do not realize they can say "no" to capitalist domination or escape from the status quo.

By echoing the pervasive disparagement of the workers, supercilious students involuntarily help to reinforce such class mistrust. The revolt of the Afro-Americans shows that the techniques of submissiveness practiced by bourgeois miseducators have limited effectiveness. The new radicals accept the fact that the black masses, so long depicted as menials, can reject their degradation, heighten their racial pride, resist their oppressors. Yet it has still to dawn on these new radicals that, at some later date, white workers too can pass through similar processes of remoralization. If black can become beautiful, so can labor in its most energetic and creative periods.

Not a few young radicals come from working-class families. Although they have come to comprehend how and why Afro-Americans have been taught to hold themselves in contempt and bend the knee to the master race and class, they fail to recognize that they can fall victim to similar pressures. Cut off from their own roots, they have been tricked into accepting the disdain for the capacities of working people inculcated by the bourgeois system.

They acquire so one-sided a view of the wageworkers by conceiving of them, not as the chief agents of production, but primarily as consumers motivated by suburbanite standards. However, the functions of the workers as purchasers of commodities are not equal in social importance to their role as the creators of wealth in the productive process. Nor do these different sides of their activities have the same weight in shaping their conduct. The reactions of the workers are primarily and ultimately determined by what happens to them in the labor market and at the point of production. That is where they encounter speedups, short time, layoffs, discrimination, insecurity, wage reductions, and other evils of exploitation. That is why any drastic fluctuation in their economic welfare can quickly alter their tolerance of the existing state of affairs.

The more sociologically inclined among the new radicals have elaborated some theoretical justifications for their disqualification of the industrial workers. They base their arguments not on the narcotizing effects of capitalist consumption and culture, but upon changes in the productive process. They point out that white-collar workers are growing faster than blue-collar workers and conclude that this relative reduction has qualitatively diminished the economic, social, and political power of the latter. Is this the case?

It is true that the labor force is undergoing marked changes in all industrial countries. Two such shifts have special significance. Because of its high capital intensity, the number of workers engaged in modern industry tends to decrease relative to the personnel employed in transport and communications, the educational system, research, government jobs, and the service trades. Further, as a result of mechanization, the percentage of technical and highly skilled workers tends to grow at the expense of the unskilled.

The implications of these structural changes in the work force do not signify that the working class as such has less importance since, in fact, the sellers of labor power grow relative to the farm population, independent small proprietors, and other sectors of society. The declining role of such social strata in production and distribution enhances the weight of others. Thus the decrease of the small farmer with the growth of large-scale mechanized enterprises in agriculture is accompanied by increases in the numbers of agricultural workers; the obsolescence of the small retailer with the expansion of chain stores creates scores of thousands of commercial employees; mechanization and automation industrialize many departments of economic activity previously unaffected by wage labor. These interrelated developments extend the scope of wage-labor relations on a scale unknown in the nineteenth century.

The main meaning of these changes is that education and skill become ever more vital in the competition for jobs and the scramble for social survival and economic advancement. On the one hand, the low-paid, unskilled segments of the laboring population become more miserable, insecure, ground down. On the other hand, the growing numbers of white-collar, professional, and technical personnel become more subjected to capitalist exploitation and alienation, more and more proletarianized, more responsive to unionization and its methods of action, more and more detached from loyalty to their corporate employers. These trends pile up combustible materials which can flare into massive anticapitalist movements.

The relative reduction in the directly producing force does not nullify the key role of the proletarians within industry. In the relations of production, quality is more decisive than quantity. Ten thousand transport workers are far more crucial in social struggle than ten thousand office workers. When 35,000 transport workers shut down the New York City subways and buses several years ago, everything ground to a halt in the hub of U. S. capitalism.

The strategic position that the mass production, transport, and communications workers occupy in the operations of capitalism invests their actions with a power exceeding their actual numbers. As direct producers, they alone can start or stop the most vital sectors of the economy. The capitalist regime is well aware of the latent power of the strike weapon wielded by blue-collar workers and constantly seeks to hamper its use. In practice, the rulers have little doubt about its revolutionary potential.

Thus one million industrial workers command incomparably more revolutionary power than seven million college students. Although the

56

three million teachers constitute the largest single occupational group in the country, their collective economic power is less than that of the half-million blue-collar workers in the steel mills.

Some envisage the imminent ejection of almost all workers from industry through the swift spread and consummation of automation. Under capitalism, mechanization and cybernation do threaten the jobs of skilled and unskilled alike, in one industry after another. The dislocations and job instability caused by these processes have to be guarded against by both the economic action and political organization of the working class.

Capitalist production cannot do without an ample laboring force, no matter how many are unemployed, because profit-making and the accumulation of capital depend upon the consumption of large quantities of labor power which creates value in the form of commodities. Although this or that segment or individual may be squeezed out of jobs temporarily or permanently, the industrial work force as such is not expendable, no matter how fast or how far automation proceeds under capitalist auspices.

Indeed, the inherent limitations upon its introduction and extension under capitalism, the inability of the profiteers fully to utilize the immense potential of the new science and technology for reducing the working day and rationalizing production, provide further reasons for breaking their hold upon industry. Socialism envisages the elimination from industry of the capitalist proprietors and coupon-clippers, rather than the workers.

In any event, the industrial workers are far from obsolescent and cannot be conjured away by abstract extrapolations. They will be on hand from now until the socialist revolution — and quite a while thereafter, because they provide the minds and the muscles for the production of all material wealth.

Marxism and the "labor metaphysic"

Two authoritative periodicals of the plutocracy, the *London Times Literary Supplement* and the *New York Times*, paid high tributes to the genius of Karl Marx on the centennial of the publication of *Capital* in 1967. It is "the most influential single work of economics ever written," said the *New York Times* editors. In the same breath they hastened to expose what in their eyes were the basic errors of Marx's teachings. Prominent among them, they insisted, was his false prediction about "the role of the working class as the gravedigger of capitalism."

"New Left" theorists play on this same theme from a different standpoint. Orthodox Marxists glorify the working class, they claim. Instead of facing up to the realities of contemporary capitalism and appraising its assimilation of the industrial workers in a dispassionate scientific manner, the disciples of Marx fall prey to what C. Wright Mills has called "the labor metaphysic." To be effective reformers of society, they ought to give up doctrinaire fascination with the leading role of the working class and look elsewhere for more suitable candidates.

They dismiss the fact that, despite the vicissitudes of the class struggle, every so often since 1917 the revolt of the workers and their allies has been victorious. Over the long run, the sum total of their successes has outweighed the reverses; the overall movement of the world working class keeps advancing toward its social goals.

The surest index to the validity of Marxism is the balance sheet of world history in this age of permanent revolution. International experience demonstrates that Marx's ideas have been vindicated over the past half-century, though only in a partial way. Like shipwrecked sailors hanging onto an overturned lifeboat in a stormy sea, all sorts of anti-Marxists cling to the fact that not all of Marx's prognoses have yet been verified, above all, in the United States. The impregnability of American capitalism constitutes their rock of salvation.

Yet they are not wholly secure even here. A not unimportant part of Marx's theory on the evolution of capitalism has already been confirmed in the United States. His forecast of the inherent tendencies of a matured capitalism to pass from competition to monopoly through the concentration and centralization of capital is epitomized by contemporary America.

What remains to be verified are the logical *political and ideological* consequences of these economic trends, namely, the transition of the workers from union to class consciousness, from bourgeois and petty bourgeois to socialist ideology, from subservience to capitalist parties to independent and militant political organization and action. The fact that these developments have been considerably retarded does not bar them from ever being realized. This very delay sets the tasks that will have to be tackled and solved in the next stage of radicalism.

The dispute between the "New Lefts" and Marxists over the role of the working class is less concerned with divergent appraisals of the facts in the present situation than with their methods of reasoning. The two proceed along different lines in analyzing the dynamics of contemporary social development. The anti-Marxists of the New Left are provincial-minded empiricists. They reject the ideas and perspectives of Marxism, not so much because these have been rendered invalid by irrefutable argument or overwhelming evidence, but because these are not yet accomplished facts.

Although they fancy themselves ahead of their contemporaries, they remain captive to the ideological and political backwardness of American life. They are swayed by the prevailing prejudices against dialectical materialism which can go unchallenged because of the absence of solid Marxist traditions and a strong socialist movement in the United States. They are hardly aware of the extent to which they have been swept along by the pragmatic habits of thought so deeply embedded in our national culture.

The hidden capacities of the oppressed

In determining whether the American working class is a dead volcano or whether explosive energies still simmer in its depths, it should be kept in mind that neither revolutionary situations nor revolutionized classes are normal occurrences. They mature at rare intervals when the slow growth of the preconditions for a showdown between contending social forces comes to a head. During the intervening lulls in mass activity, people come to believe that the social contradictions of capitalism will never generate insurrectionary moods and movements in their time.

Such a conviction became fixed in the minds of the reformists when no direct confrontation between capitalists and workers took place for fifty years from the Paris Commune of 1871 to the Russian Revolution of 1917. A like conclusion has come to the fore whenever the working class has suffered grave setbacks or passed through a protracted quiescence over the past half-century. It has taken a new upsurge or victory of the workers to dispel that defeatism.

Over the past half-century the close association of oscillations of confidence in the capacities of the working class with alternations in the intensity of the class struggle can be charted in three major waves. The pessimism produced by the collapse of the European Social Democracy in 1914 was counteracted by the triumph of the Russian workers in 1917; the catastrophic defeats of the nineteen-thirties leading to the second world war were succeeded by the revolutionary upsurge after 1943, which culminated in the Yugoslav, Chinese, Vietnamese, and Cuban victories; and the torpor of the Western working class from 1948 on was unexpectedly upset by the French general strike of May-June 1968.

Cuba shows how the urge to power can break out in the most unscheduled ways and places. Nobody in 1958 expected that a few years later the workers of that island would become uplifted by the ideals of socialist internationalism which the organizers of the July 26th Movement themselves did not then consciously hold.

Time and again funeral ceremonies performed over the revolutionism of a particular national section of the working class, or the class in general, have turned out to be premature. Such shortsightedness has resulted from an overestimation of the "reasonableness" of capitalism on the one hand and an underestimation of the latent capacities of the toilers on the other. Sudden shocks can cause the rebelliousness of the oppressed to spring to life with a celerity that confounds the skeptics and amazes the participants themselves.

Beaten down in so many ways, workers seldom suspect what they are capable of achieving under the extraordinary stimulus of a revolutionary crisis. That genius of propaganda, Tom Paine, once testified how his plunge into the First American Revolution brought forth talents hidden in him. "I happened to come to America a few months before the breaking out of hostilities . . ." he wrote some years after the Battle of Lexington. "I had no thoughts of Independence or of arms. The world could not then have persuaded me that I should be either a soldier or an author. If I had any talents for either, they were buried in me, and might ever have continued so, had not the necessity of the times dragged and driven them into action." (*Political Writings,* vol. I, 169-170)

The "necessity of the times" forces groupings, classes, and whole peoples, as well as individuals, to perform prodigious feats. The colonial rebels displayed a tenacity of purpose, unity, and skill at warfare that astonished their foe and their contemporaries, much as the Vietnamese liberation fighters have in our own day.

In a speech he made in 1968 on the fifteenth anniversary of the attack on the Moncada army garrison, Fidel Castro emphasized the immense untapped resources, lodged in the masses, that a revolution can draw upon. "The history of this Revolution has furnished us with many examples, repeated examples, of the fact that those who were in error were those who did not believe in man, that those who made the mistake and failed were those who had no confidence in the peoples, who had no confidence in man's ability to attain and develop a revolutionary awareness.

"In the past, those of us who proclaimed the revolutionary struggle, who proclaimed the need for a revolution, were told the same thing: that we were mistaken, that we were a bunch of dreamers and that we would fail.

"This was what the politicians, the 'savants' of politics, the 'professors of politics,' the 'brains' of politics, the leaders of the traditional, bourgeois parties, had to say. They did not believe in the people; they underestimated the people. They thought the people incapable of accomplishing anything. They thought of the people as an ignorant herd to be manipulated at their will. Those of you who are here today — especially those who are here as guests — and can take a good look at this enormous congregation of people which is the living expression of our Revolution's power, should not forget that only fifteen years ago we were a small group of youngsters whom many considered dreamers, who had been told they would fail because it was impossible to make a revolution in a country of illiterate, ignorant people. And yet, what is it that we see today? What has been the result of the effort begun fifteen years ago by a small group of youngsters at that stage of our revolutionary history? How much has been accomplished by this people? How much has this unarmed people accomplished? How much has this people that they called ignorant, that they underestimated, that they considered lacking in every virtue, accomplished?"

Such historical precedents suggest that the American workers ought to be sized up, not simply for what they are at a given moment, but for what they may be compelled to become under changed circumstances.

The historical judgment of the skeptics is at fault. With all its appurtenances of power, it is the corporate plutocracy rather than the proletariat that is a decaying class heading toward its demise. The American working class is fresh, vigorous, undefeated, undemoralized. It has displayed considerable fighting spirit, initiative, and stamina in the past — and its career as a creative social force has barely begun.

When republican and democratic movements first emerged in the bourgeois era, spokesmen for royalism, aristocracy, and clerical domination argued that common people were unfit to be entrusted with affairs of state. The same sort of elitist prejudice motivates some of those who today permanently preclude the workers from sovereignty in society.

On what grounds are they justified in setting arbitrary and insurmountable limits to the creative capacities of American labor? If the workers can produce airplanes and precision instruments for the industrialists and militarists and all kinds of commodities for the market, if they can build and maintain powerful industrial unions for themselves, why can't they go beyond all that?

What prevents them from organizing a mass political party of their own, being won over to socialist ideas, and eventually manning a revolutionary movement which can challenge the existing order and lead the way to a new society? Why can't these workers, who make such a plenitude of other things, also make history and remake society and, in the process, remake themselves? If they perform all kinds of jobs for the profiteers, why can't they do their own jobs? If they wage and win wars for the imperialist rulers, why can't they conduct a civil war in defense of their own interests, as their predecessors did in the nineteenth century?

The wageworkers are no more fated to remain servants in their own house than the American colonists were condemned to remain subjects of the British Crown, or the slaves to remain the property of the Southern planters. If a few million workers and a mass of illiterate peasants in less developed lands have succeeded in revolutionizing themselves along socialist lines, what inherent qualifications did they possess that the better-equipped American workers cannot acquire? The class struggle within the United States should give an answer to these questions before this century is over.

The problem of leadership

The capacities and conduct of a class at any given time depend in no slight degree on the character of its leadership. If the American workers have such a poor record over the recent past, the responsibility rests more with the men at their head than with their own inadequacies. The potentially most dynamic body of workers in the world has the most corrupt, servile, and obtuse official union leadership.

These leaders kowtow to the corporations and the government while lushly living on munificent salaries and expense accounts. They think more like big businessmen than representatives of a progressive social force. They cannot inspire the members of their organizations to higher levels of achievement in industry or politics or teach them anything new. They are rightly despised by young rebels on the campuses and distrusted and held in contempt by young workers in the plants.

Many mistakenly believe that this breed of leaders faithfully and fully represents the caliber of their ranks, that it is the only kind they can produce or follow. Actually, these officials are the product and the promoter of a prolonged period of stagnation. A resurgent labor movement would thrust forward a new type of leadership from below, and even prod some susceptible bureaucrats, as it proved capable of doing during the industrial union drive of the nineteen-thirties. Under a comparable radicalization, labor can both reenergize itself and renew its leadership.

And one thing may be anticipated. Once their militancy revives on a large scale, the American workers will travel at jet-plane speed. They will take off from the point where their march was halted and thrown back several decades ago. The mass production workers did not go ahead to form an independent political organization after they created the industrial unions in the nineteen-thirties. They were prevented from taking this next step by the John L. Lewis-Communist Party coalition in the CIO. They have suffered heavily ever since from this failure to disengage from the two big capitalist political machines.

When they again rise up, the fighting vanguard of the union movement will have to seek the road of independent political action to promote their objectives, as workers elsewhere have already done. However, they will not duplicate the precise course of political development taken by their predecessors. They will follow an exceptional line of march because their thrust toward independence comes so late on the scene, is directed against the most formidable and ruthless adversary, will be objectively intertwined with the revolutionary struggle for Afro-

American liberation, and will have been preceded by a new, radicalized generation of college and high school students and young workers. The most advanced workers will be inclined to adopt the best methods of militant action and revolutionary organization available to them.

The sharpness of their break with the old ties can impel this vanguard to make a big leap in their ideas and activity in relatively short order. Whereas the workers who were radicalized at earlier dates in other countries were attracted to Social Democratic, Fabian, or Stalinist programs and parties, these movements have today become largely discredited and decrepit. They cannot provide a new generation of rebellious workers with the leadership, organization, and program they need in the harsh struggle against the monopolists, militarists, and union bureaucracy. These militants will be open to the acceptance of the ideas of authentic Marxism, which the Trotskyist movement alone presents in the United States.

The American working class has colossal tasks ahead of it. It confronts the most formidable and ferocious of adversaries in the monopolist-militarist combine that controls American capitalism. Yet it possesses the potential of a giant. Like Gulliver, it has been pinned down by lilliputians while it has fallen into a drugged sleep.

This class will be roused from its slumber by events beyond anyone's control. Marxists do not believe that the popular masses can be summoned into battle on anyone's command. The class struggle unfolds with a rhythm of its own, according to internal laws determined by weighty objective historical conditions.

On the other hand, Marxists are neither fatalists nor anarchists. They recognize that the working masses can launch mighty offensives on their own initiative once capitalism goads them into action. It occurred to no one that February 23, 1917, would be the first day of the Russian Revolution or that May 13, 1968, in France would see the start of the greatest general strike in working-class history.

The revolutionary program and perspectives of Marxism are predicated upon fusing such autonomous actions of the masses with the conscious intervention of its socialist vanguard. The correct combination of these factors is the only guarantee of success in the combat against capitalism.

If it is not correctly oriented in time, the most powerful spontaneous upsurge can fall short of its mark, dribble away, be turned back and crushed. This misfortune has befallen the workers' movement many times over the past century.

The revolutionary party helps workers take full advantage of their opportunities in good times or bad. That is its reason for existence. Just as every army has its training camps, officer corps, and a high command, so every serious revolutionary movement needs experienced cadres of militants and a dependable general staff. Such a leadership cannot be created overnight. It should be assembled, tested, and tempered in the preparatory period of a revolutionary process. Otherwise, it may be too late. Default on this score has ruined many promising openings for the conquest of power.

The American workers will have to be morally and ideologically rearmed in order to conduct an effective struggle to the end against their exploiters. As every teacher and student knows, self-confidence is necessary to learn new skills and perform greater tasks. Any vanguard that aspires to prepare a revolutionary change in the United States will have to impart assurance to the working people that they have what it takes to meet and beat the ruling rich and liberate themselves.

This is a reciprocal process. The revolutionary socialist party enhances its own confidence to the extent that the masses it proposes to assist elevate their reliance on themselves.

The will to win is an indispensable factor in the way to win. The decisive sections of the working class, black and white, can go forward to victory only as they become convinced that the profiteers are not born to command, that they are misruling the nation and leading the world to catastrophe, that they are not omnipotent and unbeatable, that their system of exploitation is not everlasting but has to go and can be abolished. This is the essential message of Marxism. It teaches that the workers are qualified and mandated by historical progress to supplant the plutocrats as the directors and organizers of economic and political life and become the pioneers of the first truly human society.

It is obvious from these considerations that the continuing controversy over the capacities of the American working class does not involve minor issues. Nothing less than the course and outcome of the struggle for socialism and self-determination in the United States, if not the very survival of society, depend upon whether an affirmative or negative answer is given to it, first in principle, then in practice.

The Young Socialist Alliance has given the most affirmative answer to this question by its program, activities, and its very existence. You are meeting this Thanksgiving weekend to implement that faith in the potential of the American working class, black and white. Remember what Fidel Castro said last year: "Only fifteen years ago we were a small group of youngsters whom many called dreamers." You are a small group of the same sort in this country today.

But what you are and what you do here and now — and, even more, what you may become — has great political importance because you represent the vanguard of the young students and workers who are called upon to bring the liberating ideas of socialism to the American people and wipe imperialism off the face of this planet.

64

George No\

THE UNF(OF THE
NEW RADI   TION
IN THE U1   STA·TES

This article is   *peeches the author gave during a tour*
of New Zealand   *, Hong Kong, and Japan in May and*
June of 1973.

The domestic p   elopment of the United States over the
past three decades   wo distinctly different periods.

After a brief as_____ ui labor militancy in the great strike wave
from 1945 to 1947, the prolonged expansion of American capitalism and its imperialist suzerainty over most of the globe insured
the predominance of conservative attitudes in almost all areas of
life — from the ghettos to the suburbs and from philosophy to
literature.

The era of the cold war, the witch hunt, the loyalty purge, and
McCarthyism saw the wilting of liberalism and the uninterrupted
attrition of radicalism. Columbia University sociologist Daniel
Bell hailed this adaptation to the status quo as "the end of
ideology." The consensus of contentment, he explained, had ex-
pelled every serious conflict from the post-industrialized paradise
of the Yankee dollar, and all expectations of remodeling American
society, let alone revolutionizing it along socialist lines, were now
hopelessly out of touch with reality. The socialist dream had been
forever blotted out by the triumphant progress of a democratic
capitalism.

As bureaucratism tightened its grip over the unions, the ranks
of the white working class fell into apathy and immobility. Although Afro-Americans and Chicanos were deeply discontented,
their rebelliousness had not yet broken through to the surface. The
unpoliticized campus youth were dismissed as "the silent generation,"
bent on careerism within the establishment. Women, sequestered
in the nuclear family and submerged in domesticity, were least

65

of all thought of as a potential source of dissent. All the groups on the left, without exception, became more and more isolated, decimated, and unable to replenish their depleted forces. For them, this was a lost generation of recruitment.

Through the cold war years, consequently, the United States was looked upon by peoples abroad, who felt and resented its dominance, as an impregnable fortress of counterrevolution, the central powerhouse of reaction, the enemy of every progressive movement in the world. And the Vietnam war certifies that this judgment still holds true of its ruling class, despite the toasts Nixon exchanged with Mao and Brezhnev.

As it turned out, however, the glacial reaction covering the United States after 1947 was not to be everlasting and unalterable. From the early sixties on, the domestic ice cap began to break up, piece by piece, in a thaw that is far from ended.

It is instructive to trace the successive steps in the reradicalization of the country that is the consummate embodiment of monopoly capitalism. Let us review the outstanding developments as these have unfolded in the second phase of our postwar history.

The process began from below, out of the very depths of American society — among the Afro-Americans, doubly oppressed as workers and as a nationality.

Two events initiated the civil rights movement: the 1955 Montgomery, Alabama, bus boycott in the former capital of the Confederacy and the lunch-counter sit-ins of the North Carolina students in 1960. Both of these actions against racist discrimination in the Southern states were self-organized, and these initiatives in turn aroused other sectors of the black masses.

These were struggles for the simplest democratic rights, for equality of treatment in public places — the right to sit anywhere in a bus, to eat at any restaurant, to use the same toilet facilities open to whites. Almost all popular movements in history have originated on such an elementary level. Struggles for the acquisition, retention, or extension of civil liberties, ranging from the right to assemble freely to the right to strike and form unions, can mark the primary phase of mass mobilizations that eventually culminate in all-out confrontations with the existing regime.

The second development that served to revive anticapitalist ideas and sharpen anti-imperialist sentiments was the Cuban Revolution. The July 26th Movement, headed by such magnetic personalities as Castro and Guevara, proclaimed national-democratic goals. But to accomplish them the Cuban revolutionists learned that they had to carry out a socialist revolution against the mighty power of U. S. imperialism. The Cuban leaders showed their caliber in proving equal to this task. Their example evoked widespread interest and enthusiasm, especially among rebellious and alienated youth, for whom "beatnikism" had seemed the only alternative in the fifties.

Although Cuba had had its predecessors — from the October 1917 Russian Revolution to the 1949 revolution in China — these colossal upheavals had had a less direct impact upon the United States because they appeared far removed. The Cuban Revolution, however, unrolled only ninety miles from Florida and was the first to be witnessed directly by a mass audience on TV screens. (Vietnam was the second.)

The fact that this first socialist breakthrough in the Western hemisphere took place at our doorstep — and without the blemish of Stalinism — gave it more resonance than the Chinese victory ten years before. Washington's attempts to crush the Cuban Revolution, culminating in the 1961 Bay of Pigs invasion and the 1962 missile crisis, taught the new generation a lesson about the counterrevolutionary nature of U. S. imperialism. On the other hand, Cuba's expropriation of foreign and native capitalists drove home the idea that socialism was not a forlorn and utopian enterprise but a genuine option for action — in the Americas as well as Asia and Europe.

It was quite logical, after student participation in the civil rights battles in the South, the "Ban-the-Bomb" marches, and the defense of Cuba, that the next big impetus to the radicalization should come from the campuses. The student protests began at Berkeley in 1964 and spread rapidly through the United States and to other countries. A noteworthy feature of the new radicalism has been its international scope. Thanks to instant global communication, initiatives in mass protest taken in one place are quickly copied elsewhere. The sparks flying upward from one center of conflagration are whirled through the atmosphere and ignite similar actions wherever combustible materials are piled up, even in very distant regions. Thus the Berkeley Free Speech Movement, following earlier student demonstrations in Turkey, South Korea, and Japan, helped spur in its turn the youth radicalization that has since surged up on all continents.

The ten years from the Montgomery bus boycott of 1955 to the student protests of 1964 constituted the preparatory phase of the radicalization. The process was lifted to a higher level by two major developments in the mid-sixties. One was the start of antiwar mobilizations on a large scale in the spring of 1965 after Johnson's military escalation in Vietnam. The other was the growing nationalist sentiment among black Americans, expressed in the uprisings of frustrated ghetto dwellers in such big cities as Newark, New York, Washington, Detroit, and Los Angeles from 1964 to 1968.

The Afro-American fight for liberation moved from the South

to the North, from civil rights to the assertion of black nationalism and black power, from pacifist demonstrations to large-scale
clashes with the police, national guardsmen, and federal troops
that the authorities ordered in to occupy and subdue the centers
of insurgency. The representative leader of the first stage was Mar-
tin Luther King, the conciliator; the spokesman for the second was
Malcolm X, the uncompromising black nationalist opponent of the
capitalist system and its racism, whose ideas became the banner
of militancy after his death in 1965. Despite their political differ-
ences, they shared the fate of being gunned down in attempts to
behead the black movement.

Black liberation is in the forefront of the nationalist struggles
of the oppressed minorities in America. Twenty-five million Afro-
Americans are concentrated mainly in the chief cities, from the
national capital at Washington and the financial capital at New
York to the industrial metropolises of Detroit and Pittsburgh. They
comprise a majority of the inhabitants of several inner cities.

Their movement has a dual character. It fuses the democratic
thrust of an oppressed and superexploited nationality at the bottom
of the social structure with a proletarian struggle of millions toiling at the meanest and lowest-paid jobs in the service trades, industry, and agriculture. Close to one-third of the auto and steel
workers are black. That figure alone is filled with significance.

The outbursts in the ghettos were volcanic but leaderless. They
expressed an inchoate rebelliousness that continues to simmer among
the mass of blacks whose urgent needs are treated with malign
neglect. The worsening conditions in the ghettos make them a
string of time bombs ticking away in the heart of American capitalism.

The principal propellant of the radicalization from 1965 to 1973
was the antiwar movement. This was a remarkable phenomenon.
Not since the antiwar protests in Russia of 1905 and 1917 has
there been so sustained and widespread an anti-imperialist protest while the war machine of the capitalist state was carrying
on its operations.

This movement, launched by student radicals, kept mounting
until at its crest it drew the majority of the American people into
its orbit. Its spearhead was the organization of massive street demonstrations on a nonexclusionary united-front basis under the slogan
of "Bring the Troops Home Now!" The antiwar sentiment penetrated to a significant extent into the armed forces, caused divi-
sions in ruling-class circles, and restricted the maneuverability of
the president and the Pentagon in Southeast Asia. It changed the
whole political atmosphere in the country, arousing an angry resistance that drove Lyndon Johnson back to his Texas ranch.

It inspired anti-imperialist protests in other countries, from Australia and New Zealand to England and Europe.

The antiwar movement laid to rest the misconception that Americans would always line up solidly behind the monopolists and militarists and passively acquiesce in every crime their rulers committed against other nations. The size and militancy of the antiwar demonstrations in May 1970, April 1971, April 1972, and as late as Inauguration Day on January 20, 1973, showed that millions could be mobilized against the powers that be. The revelations that spilled out during the Watergate crisis disclosed that Nixon considered those antiwar forces a major threat to his administration. It is false to believe that no significant internal opposition can rise up in the happy hunting ground of the big business interests. Disneyland does not mirror all of America.

The Afro-American struggles helped spur the emergence of similar movements among other oppressed nationalities. The most sizable is that of the Chicanos, the millions of Mexican-Americans situated in the Southwest from Colorado to California, and reaching as far as the slums of Chicago and the beet fields of Michigan. The Chicanos want school instruction in their own language, development of their own culture, equal treatment and opportunity. Their symbolic rallying ground is Aztlan, the land stolen by the U.S. from Mexico under the treaty of Guadalupe Hidalgo in 1848.

Their movement, which began years later than that of the Afro-Americans, has gone beyond it in one salient respect. Blacks have yet to form a party independent from the political machines of their oppressors. More than 90 percent of Afro-American voters cast ballots for the Democratic candidates in the last three federal campaigns, and almost all their political leaders are striving to carve out local, state, and national careers within that framework.

In Texas and Colorado, however, Chicanos have launched La Raza Unida parties that have made serious showings in municipal and state elections. If they stay on an independent course and grow stronger, they have a chance of dealing a heavy blow to the political monopoly of the twin capitalist parties.

The resurgence of the Native Americans has been one of the most dramatic of the nationalist awakenings. The descendants of the victims portrayed in Western movies, on TV, and in pulp fiction have turned upon the victors and begun to demand retribution for all the crimes committed against them over hundreds of years. The second Battle of Wounded Knee, which saw two killed, climaxed a series of take-overs by Native American militants, stretching from Alcatraz Island in San Francisco Bay to Ellis Island in New York harbor.

Striking bus drivers, Pittsburgh, 1973.

Another nationalist movement involves the Puerto Ricans, who form a growing pool of low-wage labor in several Northern cities from Boston to Chicago. Already more than a million and a quarter Puerto Ricans live in New York City alone and their numbers are increasing as more leave their island home which, suffering from colonialist underdevelopment, can provide no work for them.

A central demand of the vanguard in all these movements is the cry for self-determination, for control over all the institutions in their own communities, from the schools to the police. These minorities don't want to be harried and harassed by what they look upon as the alien occupying forces of the white authorities.

The nationalist movements have tended to become polarized between the militants in the front line and the respectable reformist compromisers tied in with the capitalist establishment and ready to settle for its handouts. This by and large coincides with age levels, the elders being inclined to oppose and deprecate direct actions while their sons and daughters, affected by the youth radicalization, are no longer willing to tolerate the old state of affairs. They are intent on changing their situation "by any means necessary," as Malcolm X phrased it.

Toward the end of the sixties, women's liberation suddenly surfaced. Some groupings on the left have yet to catch on to the historical, social, and political import of the second wave of feminism. For half a century, after women won the right to vote in 1919, feminism as an organized force had been dormant. Then, starting among the New Left women on the campuses, it swelled up and swept through the country with amazing speed. Every institution now has to reckon with its presence and influence. Even the major political parties were obliged to consider the demands of women and make room for their representation at the 1972 conventions.

The subordinated sex is on the march and has already scored an impressive victory in wresting the right of abortion from a conservative Supreme Court. The attainment of this legal right against the opposition of the Catholic hierarchy augurs well in the fight for their next objectives.

Gay liberation came forward about the same time as women's liberation—and not by coincidence. The two movements have been linked together partly because one of the issues confronting women's liberation at its start was the part to be played by the lesbians in it and the attitude to be taken toward them, and partly because both challenge the distortion of sexuality and sex roles in class society. The appearance of an organized public movement of male and female homosexuals resisting their victimization and calling for recognition of their rights as human beings is one index of the extent and depth of the radicalization. It has roused hitherto unheard-from layers of the oppressed and impelled them into activity to rectify long-smoldering grievances.

The general unrest has even spread to formerly faithful and obedient Catholics, including dissident nuns and priests. It has been remarked that the Catholic church in the United States is threatened with a nervous breakdown.

Over the past three years the ranks of the rebellious have been joined by prison inmates, who are mostly young and poor Afro-Americans, Chicanos, and Puerto Ricans, often driven to crime by hopeless deprivation and victimized by cops and judges. According to a *New York Times* report, 30 percent of the current prisoners are Vietnam veterans. The whole world knows of the appalling events at Attica prison in upstate New York, where forty-three inmates and guards they held as hostages were slaughtered on orders from Governor Rockefeller. Yet this massacre is only one among scores of protests and uprisings from the East to the West Coast in prisons that seethe with the same resentments as the ghettos.

Prison rebellions nowadays have a politicized character. Many of the leaders and participants consciously identify with the Third World revolutions, the Puerto Rican, Chicano, and Afro-American struggles, and with socialism. As in czarist Russia, the prisons have become universities for the most desperately oppressed elements of society. Malcolm X, who secured his education in prison, was the forerunner of thousands of prisoners today who read what revolutionary publications they can get in their cells and discuss the ideas of Malcolm, George Jackson, Marx, Lenin, Trotsky, Mao, and others while taking recreation in the yard.

As another consequence of the radicalization, a large percentage of the young, under the impact of the Vietnam war, the youth culture, and TV, have become politicized earlier than any previous generation. Great numbers of high school students turned out for the antiwar demonstrations, and the most aggressive began pressing for more democratic rights within their schools. They carry the ferment of unrest with them, whether they go on to college or immediately enter the work force, and this should reduce the possibility that the radicalism of the sixties will run out of steam in the seventies.

During the deep freeze of the fifties, artistic experimentation and subdued liberalism were the farthest outposts occupied by the intellectuals. Beginning with the 1965 Vietnam teach-ins and the formation of the Socialist Scholars Conference, the academic community, especially in its lower echelons, began to join the student and antiwar movements. The more sensitive literary and cultural critics also fell in step with the new mood and began to ask, in Norman Mailer's words: "Why are we in Vietnam?"

The ideas of Marxism, which had been banished as subversive or branded as irrelevant, were reluctantly admitted as suitable material for college courses, while socialist, communist, and New Left speakers were invited to campuses. By the early seventies the hitherto placid annual meetings of numerous learned societies were ruffled by a clamor for reforms from radical, black and women's caucuses. Commercial publishers found profit in bringing out books addressed to a radical readership.

These shifts in the intellectual atmosphere went along with changes in the attitudes of many Americans toward the most venerated institutions. The Pentagon Papers, Watergate scandals, and other revelations exposed the deceit and double-dealing of both Republican and Democratic administrations, weakened governmental authority, and inculcated deep distrust of the highest officials. People have become sensitized as never before to the machinations of the State Department and the CIA.

The U. S. imperialists cannot embark on another open, full-scale intervention in the colonial world without the risk of outraged domestic resistance. That is one reason why the Pentagon has decided in favor of a professional rather than a conscript army.

Thanks to the various protest movements over the past fifteen years, millions of citizens have grown accustomed to go out on demonstrations demanding attention to their grievances. Parts of the population that would never before have considered taking to the streets are resorting to direct actions when they get aroused. Symptomatic was the meat boycott in 1973, a spontaneous movement against the soaring cost of living that welled up almost overnight among housewives from one end of the country to the other.

The antiwar movement adopted the principle of not excluding anyone for their ideas or affiliations, considering this principle indispensable for democratic decision-making. This greatly reduced the practice of red-baiting, that pestilential inheritance from McCarthyism. Moreover, Washington's new friendliness toward Peking and Moscow makes it harder for reactionaries to incite credible anticommunist hysteria.

Despite cries for "law and order," the government failed to secure convictions in its highly publicized persecutions of antiwar activists, such as the Harrisburg case involving the Berrigan brothers. Prosecutors have bemoaned the "revolt of the juries" as their frame-up cases against Angela Davis and other radical figures have been rejected. The hostility toward the repressive role of the police has percolated from the black communities into the attitudes of young people generally. Many have been imbued with an internationalist outlook that has made them responsive to appeals for solidarity with the Vietnamese freedom-fighters, the Palestinians, black South Africans, and Latin American political prisoners.

In spite of this impressive array of forces at odds with the status quo, it appears to some that the current radicalization is not so deep-going and durable as its predecessors. They argue that thus far it has involved only peripheral sectors of American society and, unless and until the organized workers join the fray and take its lead, it lacks substantial weight and serious significance.

These critics make two mistakes. They underestimate the depth and scope of the radicalization, and they try to squeeze its path and process of development into an arbitrary pattern prescribed by the past.

Today's radicalization is a variegated expression of the decay of monopoly capitalism and the difficulties of American imperialism. The deterioration in the quality of life and the frightful disparities in living conditions reproduce in increasing measure the discontent that feeds its growth. It has already become the most profound and extensive radicalization in twentieth century America, reaching new population sectors and geographic areas untouched by previous upsurges. Nor is it an episodic phenomenon that blazed up like a brush fire and will as quickly die down.

To be sure, the radicalization experiences ebbs and flows and its progress to date has been extremely uneven. The movement of each of the components, from the blacks to the women, has an autonomous aspect and acts in consonance with its own grievances, impulses, and situation. While each segment of the oppositional forces exerts some influence on and is influenced by others, resulting in a sharing of methods of action, their activities remain by and large uncoordinated and their aims are not promoted through any single central leadership. The most advanced elements among them momentarily came together only during the biggest national antiwar actions as contingents bearing their own banners.

The millions in ferment still constitute a minority. A radicalization is not a revolutionary or even a prerevolutionary situation any more than the prologue of a drama is the climax. It is only a precondition and preparation for future mobilizations that can more effectively challenge the possessors of power. Nonetheless, the legions of dissidents have projected a new course for the present generation and impressed a distinctive mark upon it.

It is still insufficiently appreciated that the United States is no longer simply the stronghold of world reaction but is also becoming an innovator and pacemaker in various branches of radicalism. Here is the home of the most dynamic and explosive nationalist movement of the oppressed within an imperialist center. Taking inspiration from Africa, the struggle for black liberation has in turn stirred emulation in unlikely places, as in the emergence of the "Black Panthers" in Israel. The student revolts, the Vietnam antiwar mobilizations, women's liberation, and gay liberation have all circulated from North America to other areas of the globe. The United States is serving as a laboratory for novel experiments in radical activity, all emanating from revulsion against the evils of the most highly developed capitalism.

This reedition of radicalism has not and could not duplicate the upheaval of the thirties. It originated under very different national and international circumstances and at a higher stage of monopolist evolution. It was not depression-born but took shape during a boom, growing out of multiform dissatisfactions with the effects of monopolist rule upon the everyday lives of the American masses — the reality that belied the promises of the capitalist propagandists.

The United States is a land of violent contrasts not only in its geography but in its social structure. On the one hand, superior technology, productivity, and living standards make it the wealthiest, strongest, and most stable of all the capitalist nations. On the other hand, its people have the most stunted political development and immature social consciousness in the Western world. It is quite natural that oppositional tendencies springing to life in such a peculiar milieu should display unconventional characteristics and flow through fresh channels.

The massive movement of the workers in the nineteen-thirties was preceded and prepared for by expressions of protest from intellectuals, farmers, unemployed, and youth. But by 1934 it was clearly evident that the workers had come to the fore, and they dominated the scene for the rest of the decade.

This time the Afro-Americans, students, Chicanos, Native Americans, Puerto Ricans, and women began to confront the established order while labor was still lulled by prosperity. They have had the arena to themselves for a prolonged period, and this helps account for the unique forms of the current radicalization.

The working class is the decisive social and political power in the anticapitalist struggle. Its absence in the main from the arena has restricted the radicalization, weakened its impact, and kept it incomplete. It should be borne in mind, however, that the insurgent nationalisms are a complex and compound expression of the most exploited layers of the work force — and thus an integral aspect of the class struggle.

American workers present a puzzling phenomenon because of their sharply contradictory characteristics. Well educated, highly skilled and productive, and powerfully organized in the basic industries, the tens of millions in their ranks have in the past shown themselves capable of tremendous combativeness on the economic level.

And yet, because of special historical circumstances and privileges, the ideological development and political organization of the working class lag far behind the ripeness of the American economy for socialization, and far behind the consciousness of workers in other lands. Ours is the only labor movement in the major industrialized nations that has not established a mass working-class political party. For instance, in Canada, where many of the workers belong to the same international unions (steel, lumber, auto, teamsters, electrical workers), there is a labor party—the New Democratic Party. Despite its reformist social-democratic program, the fact that there exists a mass workers' party represents an advance for the workers in Canada; in the United States the working class remains tied to the capitalist Democratic and Republican parties.

Owing to the unparalleled postwar boom, the organized workers have remained relatively quiescent for almost a quarter of a century. The steel workers have not struck since 1959 and in March 1973 their union's executive board signed a three-year no-strike agreement (over rank-and-file protests). In recent years there has been more motion among the less industrial portions of the wage earners. Most noteworthy has been the rapid expansion of unionization and strike action among public employees of diverse categories. There are more than three million teachers in the United States. Their salaries have been falling far behind the soaring cost of living while their demands have been resisted by city officials with shrinking budgets. Since the militancy of such salaried workers immediately clashes with state authority, their dozens of walkouts have tended to assume a sharp political edge.

Up to now the radicalization has affected working people mostly as Afro-Americans, Chicanos, veterans, youth, women, or consumers—but not yet in their capacity as workers, in the centers of production where it counts the most. There have been some portents of change, however. Younger workers at the General Motors Vega plant in Lordstown, Ohio, and at the Chrysler plant in Detroit, for example, have initiated some very militant battles in reaction to the inhuman speedup of the auto lines and against compulsory overtime.

Because the labor leadership is so bourgeois-minded, bureaucratic, corrupt, and conservative—and because U. S. unionism remains without any independent political representation, Marxist traditions, or socialist inspiration—some ideologues of the left and New Left have concluded that the American proletariat, bought off by the consumer society and hamstrung by prejudice and privilege, must be forever disqualified as a potentially revolutionary factor and as the prime agency of social change.

76

This pessimistic judgment negates the analysis of the contradictions of capitalist development and the estimate of the historical role of the working class made by Marxism. How well founded is such pessimism?

It is of course necessary to recognize the sluggishness of the organized workers compared with other forces. Socialists have had to adjust to this unpleasant reality for a long time. But it would be shortsighted to regard the state of the majority of the American workers in a given period, even a protracted one, as definitively fixed. Specific objective conditions generated and sustained this inertia; new conditions will undermine and alter it. After the shakeup of the Great Depression and the revival of industry, the passive working class of the nineteen-twenties became transformed into the battalions of industrial unionism that beat back the attacks of the corporations and demolished the open shop in basic industry.

The potential of today's working class for a comparable reawakening is fully intact. Labor is like a sapling bent low and tethered to the ground that could release immense energy once its bonds are broken and it springs upward.

The radicalization has already shaken the complacency of the country, alarmed its rulers in the White House, and set weighty forces in motion. But it is a long way from maturation. Its further prospects depend in large measure upon a resurgence of militancy in the ranks of labor. The economic setting for this is already in the making. Except for a brief period of economic upswing in 1971-72, coming after the recession of the previous two years, the real wages of American workers have been frozen since 1965 — since the beginning of the escalated U.S. attack on Vietnam with its inflationary consequences. Today workers face the most rapid rise in food prices in this century.

For the moment they are stunned and their forward movement is stifled by the class-collaborationist bureaucracy of the trade unions. But this set of new economic and social conditions can spur the drowsy giant to embark on large-scale offensives against the corporations that will change its ideas and outlook and raise its political consciousness to a higher level. In the process of regaining its freedom of action, labor will have to push forward a new leadership from below and boot into retirement most of the bureaucrats now heading the unions.

Its behavior over the past twenty-five years is not the most reliable key to labor's future. The question that ought to be asked is this: If so much discontent with the capitalist regime has been rife during the biggest boom in its history, what can be expected to happen as that superheated prosperity cools down and darker economic prospects pervade the land?

Following Nixon's entente with the Chinese and Soviet leaderships, his withdrawal of troops from Vietnam, his sudden turn to wage controls and dollar devaluations, and the appearance of unbridled inflation, the United States has moved into a third phase of its postwar history. While it is too soon to discern or define in detail what effects this next period will have on our lives, one point should be kept in mind.

This era is subject to abrupt turns that confound the prophets. The reversal of Nixon's economic course in 1971 and his missions to Peking and Moscow in 1972 surprised many people — not least the believers in the revolutionary anti-imperialist virtues of Mao. Then, when the president himself thought he had four years of clear sailing for his unrestrained rulership in the White House, the Watergate crimes and conspiracies exploded in his face, spattered it with mud, and severely compromised his administration.

Nor can adroit diplomatic maneuvers counteract the fact that the international financial and political power of the imperialist colossus has passed its peak. After 1945 American corporate capitalism set out with almost unlimited means to dominate the world and capture its markets. For two decades its efforts were highly successful. Now it has to steer through a minefield of obstacles: the presence of the workers' states, armed with hydrogen weapons (however much they are disarmed by the policies of their leaders), the resistance of the colonial peoples, rougher competition from European and Japanese industry, the decline of the once almighty dollar, and the specter of a generalized recession.

When the United States became the receiver in bankruptcy of the older empires, it took over more liabilities than assets. Vietnam, which Washington sought to grab after the French defeat, is a case in point. In its expansion, American imperialism has incorporated into its own structure all the unresolved problems of class society on a world scale. For all their arrogance and wealth, the monopolists are finding that these are too much for them to handle. If the rulers of this country proved unable to raise up the standards of the oppressed nationalities within their own borders during twenty-five boom years, how can they hope to meet the demands of the whole Third World? It is an impossible task.

The loss of public confidence in the leaders of the capitalist regime is a great gain for their opponents. It adds fresh fuel to the radicalization and brightens the prospects for the growth of the socialist movement in the United States. Its revolutionary vanguard is represented by the Socialist Workers Party and the Young Socialist Alliance, which have replenished and rejuvenated their forces by participating in activity and discussion in all areas of the radicalization.

The anti-Marxists insist that the ideas of scientific socialism are outmoded and inapplicable to the United States, unsuitable for either the traditions or the psychology of the American people. Such references to the immortality of national peculiarities are the last line of defense thrown up by ideological champions of the established order. They argue that because Marx worked out his theory of capitalist economic development in the British Museum and singled out nineteenth century Britain as the prime example of the contradictions of the system, his analysis is not relevant to contemporary America.

A hundred years later, however, the United States, which has displaced Great Britain as the supreme power of the capitalist world, exemplifies the laws discovered by Marx in no less striking — and far more mature — ways. The concentration and centralization of capital in giant multinational monopolies, banks, and insurance companies; the dwindling of small farming, devoured by agribusiness; the expansion of the wage-earning class beyond all others; the gap between rich and poor — all testify to the foresight and validity of Marx's political economy.

It is true that the full and final results of the inexorable operation of the laws of capitalism have yet to be brought into play on American soil. Still to be realized are the ideological and political consequences of these ongoing social and economic processes. The special course of its historical evolution, and the privileged place the United States has up to now enjoyed in the imperialist age, have tremendously retarded the emergence of these superstructural aspects in our national life.

But what is late in arriving, and even much overdue, will not forever be absent. We Marxists are not "waiting for Godot" in anticipating and preparing for the coming of a reradicalized working class and a revitalized mass socialist movement. The rise of the radicalization that succeeded the cold war reaction is a harbinger of their advent.

79

OTHER BOOKS AND PAMPHLETS BY THE AUTHORS

Ernest Mandel

Decline of the Dollar 1.75
Europe versus America 2.25
The Formation of the Economic Thought of Karl Marx 3.25
Introduction to Marxist Economic Theory 1.25
Marxist Economic Theory (2 volumes) 7.90
The Marxist Theory of the State .60
Peaceful Coexistence and World Revolution .60
The Revolutionary Student Movement .85

George Novack

Democracy and Revolution 2.95
Empiricism and Its Evolution 2.45
Genocide Against the Indians .60
How Can the Jews Survive? .25
Humanism and Socialism 2.25
Introduction to the Logic of Marxism 1.95
Marxism versus Neo-Anarchist Terrorism .25
Origins of Materialism 2.95
Revolutionary Dynamics of Women's Liberation .25
Understanding History 2.45

Ernest Mandel and George Novack

The Marxist Theory of Alienation 1.45

Available from

PATHFINDER PRESS, 410 WEST STREET, NEW YORK 10014
Write for a free catalog of other books and pamphlets on Marxism,
women's liberation, Black and Chicano studies, labor history,
Latin America, the Middle East, and current issues.